Jamie's Foreword

It's never been more important to teach our children how to cook and how to feed themselves well. Obesity has reached epidemic levels —it's a global problem that costs us billions of pounds when it comes to treating diet-related disease.

The work of Charlton Manor Primary School is setting a fantastic example of how to educate pupils about the impact of food on our health and wellbeing. Head Teacher Tim Baker, The Food Teacher, Katharine Tate, Marie Reynolds, his staff, and the pupils have created a brilliant book here. Schools and local authorities need all the help they can get, and this book contains brilliant ideas for lesson plans that bring food into every part of the curriculum.

Charlton Manor Primary will always have a special place in my heart — it was a school I first visited during my School Dinners campaign in 2005. And it was one of the first schools to develop ways of using food education to deliver the national curriculum. When I visited the school ten years later I was so incredibly impressed by the level of food understanding and the cooking skills the children had developed.

Let's spread the joy of good food, happy cooking guys!

Jamie Oliver, MBE

SUGAR SMART

Acknowledgements

I would like to thank Amy Goold my Deputy for helping with the lesson plans. To all the staff at Charlton Manor for their part in creating the health ethos particularly around food.

Thanks also to Marie Reynolds for her expertise in writing and mapping the lesson plans.

Thanks to Katharine Tate, The Food Teacher for her content contribution and project management of the book.

Thanks also to Penny Bird and Camera for the wonderful pictures. Also thank you to Sue Tate for proofreading.
And finally thanks to Nick Hussain for his outstanding design work.

Disclaimer

First published in Great Britain by Charlton Manor Primary School, Katharine Tate, The Food Teacher and Marie Reynolds in 2017.

Contents

Introduction

This book has been written as a tool for teachers. It reflects the good practice here at Charlton Manor Primary School where food is thoroughly enjoyed as a common language and employed as a means to engage children actively in their own learning.

Charlton Manor School is based in South East London in an area of deprivation. As Head Teacher, I established a healthy ethos, in particular around healthy eating, which encompasses all aspects of school life. This development was initiated by meeting Jamie Oliver several years ago when he visited our school and in response to both the ever-growing issue of childhood obesity and to increase levels of pupil engagement and motivation.

Childhood obesity has reached epidemic proportions, and society as a whole has its part to play. Charlton Manor has integrated food education throughout its curriculum ensuring that children understand the importance of knowing where their food comes from, what foods are healthy and why, how to grow their own food and how to cook and prepare healthy meals. This is delivered through a creative curriculum ensuring that each topic/unit of work includes a healthy food element and develops cooking skills such as mixing, weighing, reading recipes and using a knife.

The impact of these changes at Charlton Manor has been significant particularly around pupil engagement and enthusiasm for learning within a very purposeful, hands on theme - food.

Charlton Manor has created a food focus throughout the school and now shares this good practice nationally and internationally with schools and stake holders working in schools. We have also been fortuitous to work with some amazing names in the culinary world including Raymond

Blanc OBE, who has given a great deal of his time to developments at Charlton Manor, Levi Roots and Olivier Blanc, creator of Henri Le Worm, as well as the continued support of the Jamie Oliver team.

This book aims to support other schools who wish to follow this ethos themselves. It outlines what can be done in class and the school to develop positive food culture, how to take food education beyond the classroom, effective parental engagement and how Charlton Manor can support you further.

The book contains 28 detailed lesson plans (4 for each year group) which once taught with your children/ classes, can serve as a basis to help you consider how food can be included further in the different themes and units you teach. Each lesson contains differentiation and suggests how additional classroom support can be utilised to facilitate delivery and pupil progress. The particular lessons chosen for the book were picked predominantly by pupils who recall the buzz and excitement they experienced during their learning.

The lesson plans cover 9 different subject areas including English, Maths, Science, Art and Design, Geography and History. Each lesson plan is also linked to other cross-curricular subjects, which commonly include Design and Technology: Cooking and Nutrition.

Useful up to date web links to support delivery of the lessons can be found on the school website (www.charltonmanorprimary.co.uk).

This book has been written in collaboration with class teacher Marie Reynolds and Katharine Tate, The Food Teacher, who works with schools to educate them about the importance of food for health and well-being.

About The Head

Tim Baker has been Head Teacher of Charlton Manor Primary School for 12 years. He passionately believes that children learn best when they are engaged and enjoying what they are doing. He has found that through gardening and cooking behaviour is much improved and this impacts greatly on attainment.

Tim trained as a fitness instructor in 1986 and still runs circuit and box fit classes at a local gym. In 1992 he qualified as a children's fitness instructor and taught the 'Fit Kid' scheme at 3 gyms. The focus was to tackle the growing problem of overweight and under-active children.
Now as a Headteacher Tim is often invited to speak at conferences all over the World about Childhood Obesity and is working with many countries to tackle this issue.

Tim is a member of the National Child Measurement Program panel, The School Food Plan Alliance and the RHS Education Committee. Charlton Manor includes gardening and cooking throughout their curriculum, learning which greatly benefits the children.

How To Use This Book

This book contains four exemplar lessons with a food theme for each year group. They are usually taught as part of a unit but can be delivered as stand- alone lessons or as part of a themed day or week. While some of the lessons are approximately an hour long e.g. English and Maths, others are more realistically an afternoon e.g. Art and Science.

Each lesson is designed to build on the previous knowledge, skills and understanding of the children hence the word 'elicit' is regularly used within them. In addition, each lesson is mapped to National Curriculum. Requirements and cross-curricular links have been identified.

The format of each lesson is consistent:
Each includes a Learning Objective (learning intention) and Success Criteria (a guide which tells the learner how well they are doing). In some cases those lessons which are part of a unit require, if specified, some previous teaching and learning.

The Introduction of each lesson varies in content and approach but all serve to introduce the lessons and in many instances elicit through teacher questioning what the children already know.

The Main Teaching focuses on presenting the new material in a variety of engaging ways. Again questioning is employed as a valuable teacher tool to actively involve the children and promote good learning.

The teacher led and Independent Tasks are the activity section of the lesson, the children's opportunity to apply their learning. To cater for mixed ability class groups they are formatted into three levels of ability (BA below average, A Average and HA Higher Ability). On occasion the lessons require mixed ability groupings, as stated.

During the Plenary and AfL children get the opportunity to share their learning, reflect on it, celebrate it and evaluate it.

Suggestions are then made for Next Steps lessons and possible Home Learning opportunities.

Resources needed for the lesson are listed comprehensively and Facts for Teacher will help to inform and extend the teaching and learning where appropriate.

The see web links references throughout the plans indicate links to the school website (visit www. charltonmanorprimary.co.uk) where up to date resource links to complete and support lessons can be found.

Some lessons e.g. Mandarin can be adapted for other Modern Foreign Language lessons.

The Design and Technology Cooking and Nutrition aspect of the curriculum features heavily throughout the lessons and links to practical hands on food opportunities and learning have been identified.

Developing a Positive School Food Culture

An emphasis on food culture within a school can have the potential to make a real difference for both children and adults. At Charlton Manor we have embraced this and some good practice that could be replicated at other schools includes:

Reviewing School Food. Question the quality of the school food on offer including breakfast clubs, lunches and after school. Focus on quality nutrition, raise expectations and if necessary switch providers.

Creating a School Garden. At Charlton Manor our award-winning garden delivers numerous learning opportunities. The children grow fruit and vegetables, look after the chickens, collect the eggs, look after the bees, extract honey, recycle food waste, monitor the weather, upcycle as well as link National Curriculum targets to activities providing real experiences to embed understanding.

Creating a Teaching Kitchen. This can allow children to learn curriculum skills such as weighing, measuring, melting, changing states, dissolving, freezing as well as embedding essential cooking skills to equip them to live a healthier life.

Creating a Pupil Run School Shop. This purposeful environment allows pupils to understand the importance of factors such as money skills, addition and subtraction, profit and loss, investment, as well as targeting customers through persuasive writing to advertise or buy. Write reports about the shop. Question customers about food choice or research into pricing.

Creating a School Restaurant/Cafe. This can be established as a welcoming place that values food and allows children to sit and talk quietly in a wonderful atmosphere. Children wait on tables and learn responsibility, work ethic and support.

Creating a Community Garden. This can provide another space for children to learn and potentially work with community groups and local secondary schools to support the transition process.

Creating Parental Links. Celebrate food diversity in your school and engage parents to share their expertise around food. Invite parents into classrooms and to lunches/food events and offer food and nutrition talks and workshops to educate and support parents.

Creating Community Links. At Charlton Manor we welcome elderly vulnerable adults from the community for lunch once a week. Pupils sit with them and engage in conversation whilst other pupils wait on them. Connecting with local cafés, restaurants, food producers, allotment groups can also be invaluable.

Creating International Links. Opportunities to connect with overseas groups can enhance the curriculum further.

Lesson Overviews
Foundation & Key Stage 1

Year	Subject	Learning Objectives	Cross Curricular Links	Pages
R	Numeracy	To describe everyday objects in terms of long and short.	CLL, PD, UW, EAD	18, 19, 20
R	Literacy	To complete a line in a poem.	EAD, Phonics, PD, UW	21, 22, 23
R	Literacy	To write a healthy shopping list.	CLL, Numeracy, Phonics, PD, UW, EAD	24, 25, 26
R	Literacy	To write a menu.	CLL, EAD, Phonics, PD, UW	27, 28, 29
1	Maths	To recognise, find and name a quarter as one of four equal parts of an object or shape.	D&T: Cooking and Nutrition	34, 35, 36
1	English	To write sentences, sequencing them to form a short narrative.	Maths, Science, D&T: Cooking and Nutrition, Music	37, 38, 39
1	History	To find out how and why people in Britain grew their own food during WW2	English, Science, D&T: Cooking and Nutrition	40, 41, 42

Year	Subject	Learning Objectives	Cross Curricular Links	Pages
1	Art & Design	To explore mark-making using a variety of tools.	Science, D&T: Cooking and Nutrition	43, 44, 45
2	Maths	To measure accurately using ml.	English, Science, History, D&T: Cooking and Nutrition	50, 51, 52
2	Science	To identify sources of food (Living Things).	Geography, D&T: Cooking and Nutrition	53, 54, 55
2	History	To plan a diary entry.	Maths, English, Science, D&T: Cooking and Nutrition	56, 57, 58
2	RE	To make a hot cross bun.	Maths, D&T: Cooking and Nutrition, Science	59, 60, 61

Lesson Overviews
Key Stage 2

Year	Subject	Learning Objectives	Cross Curricular Links	Pages
3	Maths	To solve 2-step word problems using money.	D&T: Cooking and Nutrition	66, 67, 68
3	English	To write and recite a verse using alliteration.	D&T: Cooking and Nutrition	69, 70, 71
3	Geography	To learn about foods typical of Italy.	D&T: Cooking and Nutrition, ICT	72, 73, 74
3	History	To learn about the history of afternoon tea, a food tradition that is still popular today.	D&T: Cooking and Nutrition, Art, ICT	75, 76, 77
4	Maths	To find the area of rectilinear shapes.	D&T: Cooking & Nutrition	82, 83, 84
4	English	To plan a persuasive letter to the Prime Minister.	History, D&T: Cooking and Nutrition	85, 86, 87
4	Science	To find out what happens to foods when they are heated and cooled.	Maths, D&T: Cooking & Nutrition	88, 89, 90
4	Geography	To find out where our food comes from.	English, D&T: Cooking & Nutrition, Citizenship & PSHE	91, 92, 93

Year	Subject	Learning Objectives	Cross Curricular Links	Pages
5	Maths	To collect and record data. To find fractions of amounts.	English, History, D&T: Cooking and Nutrition	98, 99, 100
5	English	To research and plan a delicious and nutritious meal for a dinner party in space.	Science, Maths, D&T: Cooking and Nutrition	101, 102, 103
5	Science	To understand different methods for separating mixtures.	Maths, D&T: Cooking and Nutrition	104, 105, 106
5	Art & Design	To dye yarn using naturally made dyes.	History, Science, Maths, D&T: Cooking and Nutrition	107, 108, 109
6	Maths	To measure angles	History, English, D&T: Cooking & Nutrition	114, 115, 116
6	English	To write a recount.	History, D&T: Cooking and Nutrition	117, 118, 119
6	MFL Mandarin	To describe food from another culture.	English	120, 121, 122
6	D&T	To design and make a prototype for a chicken coup.	ICT, Science, D&T: Cooking & Nutrition	123, 124, 125

Reception Lessons

Numeracy
Literacy
Literacy
Literacy

Reception Lesson Overview

Subject	Learning Objectives	Curriculum Links	Cross Curricular Links	Page Numbers
Numeracy Bone Measurement	To describe everyday objects in terms of long and short.

To be able to order two or three items by length or height. | **ELG 12 Shape, space and measures** Children use everyday language to talk about size, weight, capacity, position, distance, time and money to compare quantities and objects and to solve problems. They recognise, create and describe patterns. They explore characteristics of everyday objects and shapes and use mathematical language to describe them. | CLL (follow directions, understand simple concepts, build vocabulary) PD (safely handle malleable materials with control) UW (how things work, e.g. the skeleton) EAD (creating representations, building repertoire of songs) | 18, 19, 20 |
| **Literacy** Senses Poetry | To complete a line in a poem. | **ELG 09 Reading** Children read and understand simple sentences. They use phonic knowledge to decode regular words and read them aloud accurately. They also read some common irregular words. They demonstrate an understanding when talking with others about what they have read.

ELG 10 Writing Children use their phonic knowledge to write words in ways which match their spoken sounds. They also write some irregular common words. They write simple sentences which can be read by themselves and others. Some words are spelt correctly and others are phonetically plausible. | EAD (exploring sound) Phonics (distinguishing sounds) PD (handling tools safely, variety of food) UW (observations) | 21, 22, 23 |

Subject	Learning Objectives	Curriculum Links	Cross Curricular Links	Page Numbers
Literacy Healthy Eating Shopping List	To write a healthy shopping list.	**ELG 02 Understanding** Pupils follow instructions involving several ideas or actions. They answer 'how' or 'why' questions about their experiences and in response to stories and events. **ELG 05 Health and self-care** Children know the importance for good health of physical exercise and a healthy diet, and talk about ways to keep healthy and safe. They manage their own basic hygiene and personal needs successfully, including dressing and going to the toilet independently. **ELG 10 Writing** Children use their phonic knowledge to write words in ways which match their spoken sounds. They also write some irregular common words. They write simple sentences which can be read by themselves and others. Some words are spelt correctly and others are phonetically plausible.	CLL (follow directions, understand simple concepts) Numeracy (Shape, Space and Measures - create and recreate patterns) Phonics (distinguishing sounds) PD (handling tools safely, variety of fruit) UW (make observations) EAD (building repertoire of songs)	24, 25, 26
Literacy Menu Writing	To write a menu.	**ELG 02 Understanding** Pupils follow instructions involving several ideas or actions. They answer 'how' or 'why' questions about their experiences and in response to stories and events. **ELG 10 Writing** Children use their phonic knowledge to write words in ways which match their spoken sounds. They also write some irregular common words. They write simple sentences which can be read by themselves and others. Some words are spelt correctly and others are phonetically plausible.	CLL (follow directions, understand simple concepts, build vocabulary) EAD (creating representations, building repertoire of songs) Phonics PD (handling tools safely, variety of food) UW (make observations of their environment)	27, 28, 29

Reception Numeracy Lesson
Bone Measurement

Theme/Unit
Ourselves

Lesson Overview
To explore and order everyday items in terms of length and height.

Learning Objectives
To describe everyday objects in terms of long and short.

To be able to order two or three items by length or height.

Success Criteria
Must: I know when items are long or short.
Should: I can order two or three items by length or height.
Could: I can explain how and why I order items by length or height.

Introduction
Begin reading Funny Bones by Janet and Allan Ahlberg and stop once you have introduced the three skeletons, the big skeleton, the little skeleton and the dog skeleton.

Explain to the children that during the lesson they are going to be looking more closely at these skeletons and you will continue reading the story afterwards.

Main Teaching

Show two skeletons, a big skeleton and a little skeleton. Elicit their names from the story and record 'big' and 'little' on the WB.

Ask the children to describe the skeletons using these words e.g. this skeleton is big, this skeleton is little.

Question the children as to why one is called big skeleton and the other is called little skeleton. Elicit the words are describing their size.

Ask if they can suggest another word for little. Record 'small' on the WB. Look again at the skeletons.

Ask the children if they can suggest other words that tell us the same thing e.g. tall skeleton and short skeleton. Elicit the words are describing their height.

Record 'tall' and 'short' on the WB and compare with big and little.

Teacher to stand up together with a child, ask if the children can use those words e.g. Miss _____ is tall. _____ is short.

Ask what else we might describe as tall. Elicit tall trees, tall buildings, tall hats...

Ask two children to stand up and compare their hair length.

Ask: Would we say _____ has big hair? Would we say _____ has tall hair? Elicit _____ has long hair.

Ask: Would we say _____ has small hair? Elicit _____ has short hair.

Record 'long' on the WB. Discuss why we sometimes use long instead of tall.

Ask the children what else we might describe as long. Elicit long hair, trousers, journey etc.

Revisit all the words on the WB. Encourage the children to read them and group them into two sets. Elicit big, tall and long in one set and small and short in the other.

Show the two skeletons again. Ask some children to make up sentences using each of these words to describe the skeletons e.g. the skeleton is big or the skeleton is tall etc.

Now introduce the skeleton of the dog.

Ask: Can the children put all three skeletons in order by length or by height?

Discuss their choices.

Teacher Led and Independent Group Tasks
Introduce a carousel of activities, explaining to the children how each one will expect them to use the mathematical language on the WB. Teacher, teaching assistant and parent helper to work with chosen groups.

Cutting and assembling: Have a selection of 3 different sized skeletons for the children to each cut out one skeleton and assemble using split pins. Once made they can compare lengths.
In the kitchen: Make bread stick bones of various lengths by rolling out dough and comparing their lengths.
Sorting: Sort a selection of the aforementioned items into sets of long/tall and short e.g. skeletons, trees, buildings, lego people, trousers etc.
Threading: Make snake skeletons by threading beads or cotton reels onto laces to make three different lengths. Can you put them in order starting with the longest?
Clay modelling: Make and arrange clay bones to make people and animal skeletons.
Revisit the mathematical language on the WB before the children begin.

Plenary (AfL Focus)
Encourage the children to share their learning e.g. those with skeletons can put them in order of height, those who sorted items can explain their choices, those who baked bread stick bones can arrange them in order of length before sharing them with the class etc.

Revisit the learning objective and self-assess their learning using Steps to Success.

Continue reading Funny Bones, pausing on occasion to elicit the word tall instead of big skeleton and short instead of small.

End with a song and dance: 'Dem Dancing Bones'.

Next Steps/Home Learning
Numeracy: Measuring everyday items using non-standard units.

Home Learning: Compare your families' foot sizes. Put them in order.

Resources/Facts for the Teacher:
Funny Bones by Janet and Allan Ahlberg, three cut out skeletons: one big, one small and one dog, WB, enough simple skeleton cutting activities for a group (3 sizes), split pins, dough and cutting boards, sorting rings, labels and items to sort (long trousers, short trousers, tall building, small building, lego adult etc.), beads, cotton reels, laces, pictures of snakes skeletons to inspire, clay/playdough, cutting boards, pictures of animal skeletons and song Dem Dancing Bones.

Reception Literacy Lesson
Senses Poetry

Theme/Unit
Ourselves

Lesson Overview
Children to compose class poems inspired by their exploration of the five senses.

Learning Objective
To complete a line in a poem.

Success Criteria
Must: I know my five senses.
Should: I can tell you what I see, hear, smell, taste and touch.
Could: I can write down my ideas.

Introduction
Read the children a poem entitled 'Wonderful World' by Eva Grant (see web links).

Discuss what it is about. Draw the children's attention to the lines: I can see, I can taste, I can hear etc.

Ask what parts of our bodies help us to do these things e.g. I can see with my eyes, I can taste with my tongue etc.

Display pictures of each body part and through questioning help them to identify the sense.

Encourage the children to sound out the words as you record the five senses on the WB.

Establish that our senses help us to make 'sense' of the world.

Main Teaching
Assign a sense per table group and give them a corresponding sticker e.g. smell has a nose sticker, taste a tongue etc. Explain that each group will work with an adult to explore that particular sense before returning to class to share what they have learnt.

'I can see' Group
Go for a walk around the school. Stop on occasion, all make binoculars and play I spy. Elicit what body part and sense the children are using to play the game. Discuss how the eyes tell the brain. Prompt the sentence 'I can see with my eyes.' Compose it together with the children on a sentence strip. Encourage them to use their phonic knowledge to help you spell the words. Add 'I can see...' on a sentence strip and ask them to suggest some things they see or like to look at. Complete the sentence using their ideas. Together read both sentences.

'I can hear' Group
Encourage the children to sit cross legged like a frog, with eyes shut, feet and hands still, listening to their breath. Tell them you are going to introduce a sound e.g. a bell ringing. Ask if they recognised the sound? Make other sounds. Elicit what body part and sense they used to help them identify the sound. Continue outside. Discuss how the ears tell the brain. Prompt the sentence 'I can hear with my ears' and 'I can hear ... '. Compose the sentences on sentence strips together and read, as above.

'I can feel' Group
Introduce a 'feely tray' of objects and encourage the children to use their hands to describe the textures. Promote descriptive vocabulary e.g. a silky ribbon, cold, slimy spaghetti, squishy marshmallow. Identify the body part and sense. Discuss how the fingers/skin tell the brain. Prompt and complete the sentences 'I can touch with my skin' and 'I can touch...' on sentence strips. Record and read.

'I can smell' Group
Visit the kitchen to smell a selection of herbs and spices. Discuss the smells e.g. mint, pepper. Hide some common smells in food containers with air holes e.g. cheese, vinegar, perfume etc. Encourage the children to identify them and describe them e.g. smelly cheese, flowery perfume. Elicit the body part and sense and discuss how the nose tells the brain. Prompt and complete the sentences 'I can smell with my nose' and 'I can smell ... '. Record and read the sentences together.

'I can taste' Group
Visit the kitchen to taste a selection of food samples e.g. honey, lemons, salted crisps, raisins, unsweetened chocolate and olives. Discuss the tastes e.g. sweet, sour, bitter, salty and yucky! Elicit the body part and sense used and how the tongue tells the brain. Prompt and complete the sentences 'I can taste with my tongue' and 'I can taste...' all the while encouraging the children to use their phonics. Record and read the sentences together.

All groups return to class and take it in turn to share their experiences and group sentences. Arrange the sentence strips on the WB to create a Five Senses Poem. Read it together.

Teacher Led and Independent Group Tasks
Remind the children of their stickers and their sense experience.

Explain how each child will now concentrate on writing a sentence for their sense poem, based on their experience. Provide props and class poem sentence strips accordingly and differentiated scaffolds.

(BA) Teaching Assistant to work with the group to further explore their given sense. Use the props to elicit what they like to e.g. see. Help them to read the relevant class sentence strip e.g. I can see with my eyes. I can see … and encourage them to each complete the sentence with their choices before trying to write it using appropriate scaffolding. Then draw a corresponding picture.

(A) Ensure each group knows which sense they are focusing upon. Encourage them to explore their sense using the props, read the sentence strips together and suggest their own endings before writing them down on given scaffolds. Then draw a corresponding picture. Teacher to work between the groups and encourage them to use their phonic knowledge to write words.

(HA) Ensure they know the sense they are focusing upon. Children to explore and record their own preferences, as above, but quite independently, using appropriate scaffolds. Then draw a corresponding picture.

Plenary (AfL Focus)
Play Hands Up: Who can name the five senses? Suggest that they rearrange themselves into 'five sense groups' i.e. move around the classroom with their poem and then sit together in a groups with see, hear, smell, taste and touch friends. Once in sense groups encourage each group to read their sentences in turn to form a group poem. Revisit the learning objective and self-assess their learning using Steps to Success. Compile poems in a class book entitled 'Our Five Senses'.

Next Steps/Home Learning
At Play: Use your sentences while next in the playground to make sense of the world outside.
Home Learning: Use your senses at home. Talk about what you notice.

Resources/Facts for the Teacher
Five Sense Poem (e.g. Wonderful World by Eva Grant), Picture cards (eyes, ears, nose, fingers, mouth/tongue), Sentence strips, A selection of sounds (e.g. bell ringing, drum beat, clock ticking), A feely tray of objects (e.g. a silky ribbon, cold, slimy spaghetti, squishy marshmallow), A selection of herbs and spices, food containers with a selection of smells within (e.g. smelly cheese, fresh mint, flowery perfume, A selection of food samples for the children to taste (e.g. honey, lemons, salted crisps), Enough sense stickers for each child to have one (i.e. in a class of 30, six of each sense), differentiated writing scaffolds.

Reception Literacy Lesson
'Healthy Eating' Shopping List

Theme/Unit
Healthy Eating through Stories

Lesson Overview
Explore healthy eating through The
Enormous Crocodile by Roald Dahl.
*Read 'The Enormous Crocodile' prior
to this lesson.

Learning Objective
To write a 'healthy eating' shopping list.

Success Criteria
Must: I know that some foods are healthy
and some are not.
Should: I can make some healthy food
choices.
Could: I understand why foods are healthy.

Introduction
Show The Enormous Crocodile book
and through questioning revisit the story.

What did the Enormous Crocodile want?
What tricks did he play on the children?
Who are the main characters?
How did they warn the children?
How do you think the children felt at the
end of the story?
How would you feel?

Explain how the school children would
like to reward the animals by inviting them
to a special lunch at their school but they
need some help planning a 'Healthy Eating
Shopping List'. Can we help them?
Do we know what foods are healthy?
Discuss.

Main Teaching

Have the children sit in a circle and elicit first what each of the characters liked to eat, explaining they are the special guests so need to be happy with their lunch e.g. Notsobig liked to eat fish, Humpy Rumpy – ? Trunky – leaves, Muggle Wump -nuts, Roly Poly Bird – ? Toto and Mary – coconuts.

Ask what they think hippopotami and birds usually eat.

Show samples/pictures of these foods and explain their health benefits e.g. fish is important for our brains, nuts are a growing food (protein) and salad leaves keep us healthy. Record the choices on the WB.

Ask the children what their favourite 'healthy' lunches are and through discussion agree on three/four possible options for the special lunch e.g. fish pie, spaghetti bolognaise etc.

Record them on the WB and explain how you will record the most popular meal by listening to each of their choices during a game and then by counting the choices on a tally chart.

Play the circle game 'I like to eat … What do you like to eat?' (i.e. a child holding a bean bag says 'I like to eat fish pie' before passing it to their neighbour and asking 'What do you like to eat?' and so on around the circle).

Meanwhile teacher records the choices on the tally chart. Once everyone has made a choice count the results together. Find the most popular lunch and then ask the children to consider its ingredients e.g. what ingredients do we need to buy to make this?

Model writing the 'Healthy Eating Shopping List' on a large sheet of paper. Listen to the children's suggestions for ingredients. Record them. Encourage them to use their phonic skills to help you spell the words.

Query how to include the character's food choices e.g. a fish soup/mackerel pate or salad with leaves, nuts and berries. What might they drink? (Coconut water perhaps?)

Complete the shopping list and read it through together. Encourage the children to consider each ingredient and ask if it is a healthy choice. If not, why not and could they suggest a healthy replacement?

Teacher Led and Independent Group Tasks

Now for dessert: Make fruit kebabs. Share with the children a selection of washed and chopped fruits and berries. Can they name each fruit? Explain how berries are good for us. They contain lots of antioxidants, which are like 'superheroes' in the body. These 'superheroes' help us to keep fit and healthy. Consider the health benefits of eating a rainbow of colours, it helps digestion and keeps the eyes and brain healthy. Choosing two/three fruits can they make a pattern with the fruits? Model some examples. Children to work in mixed ability groups, with adult supervision. Each select two or three types of fruit and plan a repeating pattern. Chat about their choices with the group. Thread the fruit onto skewers.

Plenary (AfL Focus)
Return to class and read through the 'Healthy Eating Shopping List' together.

Ask: Have we thought of everything? Are we happy that the food is healthy? Will the animals enjoy their special lunch?

Revisit the learning objective and self-assess their learning using Steps to Success. Elicit what else they have learnt from the story and sing 'Never Smile at a Crocodile'.

Enjoy eating the fruit skewers during snack time.

Next Steps/Home Learning
D&T: Cooking and Nutrition: Make mackerel pate and tomato and prawn lettuce wraps (see No Kitchen Cookery For Primary Schools by Katharine Tate).
Home Learning: Make some healthy food choices at home and ask if you can add some healthy snacks to the shopping list.

Resources/Facts for the Teacher
The Enormous Crocodile by Roald Dahl, samples/ pictures of the food the characters like (e.g. fish, leaves, nuts), bean bag, large sheet of paper for the shopping list, a selection of fruits and berries, kebab sticks, chopping boards, small knives, recipe book 'No Kitchen Cookery For Primary Schools' by Katharine Tate, Song: Never Smile at a Crocodile Song (see web links).

Reception Literacy Lesson
Menu Writing

Theme/Unit
In the Garden

Lesson Overview
Use the story 'Bog Baby by Jeanne Willis and Gwen Millward' as a stimulus to explore the importance of healthy food and shelter for living things.
Read 'Bog Baby' prior to this lesson.

Learning Objective
To write our own Bog Baby menu.

Success Criteria
Must: I know that food and shelter are important.
Should: I can suggest some healthy food choices.
Could: I can help to write a menu for Bog Baby.

Introduction
Show the children the Bog Baby book. Explain to them that they will be going on a Bog Baby hunt to the garden.

Revisit the illustration in the book to help the children describe what Bog Baby looks like and where Bog Baby might be e.g. boggly eyes and a spiky tail, floating up and down on his back etc.

Suggest they look out and listen for clues once in the garden e.g. Bog Baby noises, foot prints etc. Also encourage them to consider what food is growing in the garden that Bog Baby might eat.
Begin the hunt to find Bog Baby.

Main Teaching

Return excitedly to class with Bog Baby. Refer to the story and elicit how best to look after Bog Baby for the day in class.

1. Bog Baby will need some place to sit, nap, swim... Discuss the importance of living things having shelter. Have some netting, a jar, bucket and pictures of bluebell woods ready to use and ask the children what else they might need to collect. Elicit some natural materials such as shells, wood, twigs, leaves, moss and pebbles. Listen to their ideas.

2. Bog Baby will need to eat snacks and lunch. Discuss the importance of eating healthy food. Question the children as to what they spotted in the garden that could be used e.g. carrots, mint leaves, lettuce. Show a selection of foodstuffs the chef has in the kitchen that might be good to use e.g. jelly, passion fruit, apples, honey, raisins, eggs, flour. Show some ice cube trays, small muffin tins and ramekins. Encourage the children to think how these ingredients could be used to make healthy snacks and meals for Bog Baby. Listen to their suggestions e.g. jelly with passion fruit to look like frogspawn poured into ice cube trays, carrot cupcakes or fish pie.

3. Suggest the class plan ahead so Bog Baby can visit daily through the week. Elicit how they need to plan a menu of healthy snacks and lunches. Refer to the story to confim cake crumbs are not the answer e.g. carrot sticks, apple pieces with peanut butter etc. Remind them about what was in the garden earlier and is in the kitchen.

Listen to their suggestions. Record their ideas in note form.

Teacher Led and Independent Group Tasks

Let's prepare for Bog Baby's visits.

(BA) Teaching Assistant to work with the group to design and make a place for Bog Baby to stay when visiting. Consider the materials at hand and collect others from around the classroom and garden. Listen to their ideas and agree on a plan of action. Construct Bog Baby's home. Draw a diagram and encourage the children to use their writing skills to label it.

(A) These three groups to visit the kitchen with parent helpers. Each group to consider the ingredients and the earlier class discussion before preparing some snacks for Bog Baby e.g. carrot sticks with mint dip, apple slices with drizzles of honey and mini carrot cakes. Take photographs during the preparations, to share with the class on their return.

(HA) Teacher to work with this group to record Bog Baby's weekly menu to include snacks and lunch. Look at the class notes and remind the children of earlier suggestions made by the class. Encourage the children to record these ideas and their own, using their phonic skills to help them spell unfamiliar words.

Plenary (AfL Focus)

Children to share their learning and the food they prepared with Bog Baby and the class. Read the menu as a class.

Revisit the learning objective and self-assess their learning using Steps to Success.

Return to the garden with Bog Baby and play 'In and Out the Dusty Bluebells' before placing Bog Baby where they found him/her (see web links).

Next Steps/Home Learning
D&T: Cooking & Nutrition: Use Bog Baby's menu to plan and make lunch for Bog Baby e.g. fish pie.
Home Learning: Find out where and when you can see bluebells in the woods locally.

Resources/Facts for the Teacher
Bog Baby by Jeanne Willis and Gwen Millward. For the Bog Baby Hunt (prepare written clues e.g. Look for? and Listen for? Place Bog Baby foot prints along the route of the hunt for the children to find, hide a Bog Baby), netting, a jar, bucket and pictures of bluebell woods and access to natural materials e.g. shells and twigs, foodstuff (e.g. jelly, passion fruit, apples, honey, raisins, eggs, flour), ice cube trays, small muffin tins and ramekins, class camera.

In and Out the Dusty Bluebells (circle game- see web links for tune).
In and out the dusty bluebells, Tippy-tippy tap-toe on my shoulder,
In and out the dusty bluebells, Tippy-tippy tap-toe on my shoulder,
In and out the dusty bluebells, Tippy-tippy tap-toe on my shoulder,
Will you be my master? You will be my master.
The children stand in a circle; hands joined and held up to form an arch. As the first verse is sung a child weaves in and out through the arches. At the end of the first verse the child stops and taps on the shoulder of the nearest child. When the song begins again the new leader and the first child continue to weave in and out of the arches. As the song continues the weaving line gets longer until you stop.

Year 1 Lessons

Maths
English
History
Art & Design

Year 1 Lesson Overview

Subject	Learning Objectives	Curriculum Links	Cross Curricular Links	Page Numbers
Maths Pizza Fraction	To recognise, find and name a quarter as one of four equal parts of an object or shape.	**Ma1/2.4** Fractions Ma1/2.4b recognise, find and name a quarter as 1 of 4 equal parts of an object, shape or quantity.	D&T: Cooking and Nutrition	34, 35, 36
English Bee Lifecycle	To write sentences, sequencing them to form a short narrative.	**En1/1 Spoken Language** En1/1a listen and respond appropriately to adults and their peers En1/1b ask relevant questions to extend their understanding and knowledge En1/1e give well-structured descriptions, explanations and narratives for different purposes, including for expressing feelings. **En1/3.3 Composition** En1/3.3a write sentences by: i. Saying out loud what they are going to write about ii. Composing a sentence orally before writing it iii. Sequencing sentences to form short narratives iv. Re-reading what they have written to check that it makes sense En1/3.3b discuss what they have written with the teacher or other pupils En1/3.3c read their writing aloud clearly enough to be heard by their peers and the teacher.	Maths, Science, D&T: Cooking and Nutrition, Music, Art	37, 38, 39

s

Subject	Learning Objectives	Curriculum Links	Cross Curricular Links	Page Numbers
History Grow your Own (WW2)	To find out how and why people in Britain grew their own food during WW2.	**Hi1/1.2** events within living memory that are significant nationally or globally **Hi1/1.3** significant historical events, people and places in their own locality.	English, D&T: Cooking and Nutrition, Science	40, 41, 42
Art & Design Fruit and Vegetable Portraits	To explore mark-making using a variety of tools.	**Ar1/1.1** to use a range of materials creatively to design and make products **Ar1/1.3** to develop a wide range of art and design techniques using colour, pattern, texture, line, shape, form and space **Ar1/1.4** about the work of a range of artists, craft makers and designers, describing the differences and similarities between different practices and disciplines, and making links to their own work.	Science, D&T: Cooking and Nutrition	43, 44, 45

Year 1 Maths Lesson
Pizza Fractions

Theme/Unit
Fractions

Lesson Overview
To explore quarters
of a shape using pizzas.

Learning Objective
To recognise, find and name a quarter
as one of four equal parts of an object
or shape.

Success Criteria
Must: I know what a quarter is.
Should: I can find a quarter of a shape.
Could: I can use quarters to solve simple
problems.

Introduction
Revisit previous learning about ½'s, as two
equal parts of a whole.

Teacher to show a large circle of paper.
Call it a whole circle or a whole pizza.

Write 'whole' on the shape.

Encourage the children to look at the shape
and describe it e.g. flat, no corners and one
curved side.

Teacher to begin folding it and elicit from
the children what you are doing e.g. folding
it in half so each piece is equal.

Consider the word 'half' and ask if anyone
knows another way of writing half e.g. ½.

Encourage some children to come and
model writing it on the WB. Can they
explain ½ (i.e. one whole shape folded
into two)?

Ask them to look at the new shape and
describe it e.g. flat, smaller, two sides, a
straight side and a curved side. Write ½
on each half of the shape.

Open the shape out and ask how many
halves in a whole pizza? Show a real pizza.
Tell them that you and your friend often
share a pizza. Ask how they would cut it
so you each get an equal piece. Choose
a child to cut it in half? Evaluate.

Record ½ + ½ = 1 whole

Main Teaching

Give each child a paper circle. Ask them to fold it in two equal halves and label each ½. Suggest they open out the shape into a whole again. Ask how many ½'s there are in the whole. Ask are they equal?

Show them the real pizza again and explain how there are four people in your family who like pizza so cutting it into two equal pieces will mean two people won't have any. Ask can they help you solve the problem. Work together using the whole circle again.

Ask the children to fold the circle in half /two equal pieces so they can't see the labels saying ½. Teacher to model using a large circle. Elicit that you could fold the shape again. Encourage them to consider the new shape and describe it e.g. flat, smaller, three sides, two straight sides etc.

Ask if anyone knows the name of this piece of pizza. Tell the children it is called a quarter and is written ¼. Have them write ¼ on that piece and then open their circle to see if there are any more quarters. Establish that there are four equal pieces and each is called a ¼. Encourage the children to label them in ¼'s.

Ask for a volunteer to solve your real pizza problem, cutting up the pizza into ¼'s. Evaluate. Record ¼ + ¼ + ¼ +¼ = 1 whole. Use the pizza slices to question the children and reinforce their learning: How many ¼'s are there in a whole pizza? Will there be enough for each person in the family? If Dad eats early because he is going out, how many ¼'s will be left? If Mum is not feeling well and gives her piece to you, how much pizza do you eat?

Teacher Led and Independent Group Tasks

Ask the children what toppings they like on their pizzas. Explain that in another lesson they will be making pizzas but first they must plan and design their pizza using what they have learnt about ¼'s. Introduce the Menu cards. Suggest they each choose the Menu Card of the pizza they'd like to make. Follow the instructions to plan and design their own pizza using ¼'s.

(BA) Teaching Assistant to work with the group to help them to design their pizzas. Firstly talk through the learning using their paper circles: Show me a whole pizza. Fold it so you can share it between yourself and your friend. How much of the pizza do you get to eat? Use your paper pizza to show how a family of four would share out the pizza equally. What is each piece called? Talk through their pizza choices, making sure they understand the instructions before drawing toppings and labelling.

(A) Working quite independently, aim to follow the instructions on a Menu Card to design your pizza. Teacher to move between the groups.

(HA) As above but working independently.

Plenary (AfL Focus)
Display one of each Menu Card and talk through the ingredients. Children to share their pizza plan using mathematical language (¼'s, ½'s, ¾'s and whole). Can the other children work out which pizza they have designed?

Revisit the learning objective and self-assess their learning using Steps to Success.

Next Steps/Home Learning
D&T Cooking and Nutrition: Make the pizza dough and decorate your pizza according to your plan.
Maths: Continue with pizza theme to explore quarters as four equal pieces of a quantity e.g. The pepperoni pizza has 8 pieces of pepperoni on it, how many will be on each ¼?

Resources/Facts for the Teacher
Make Menu Cards, 2 large circles of card, enough paper circles for each of the children, a pizza, pizza plate and cutting tool.

Suggestions for Menu Cards
Pepperoni Pizza - Put olives on ¼ of the pizza, put pepperoni on ¾s of the pizza. Sprinkle the whole pizza lightly with cheese.

Margarita Pizza - Put tomatoes on ½ of the pizza, put basil on 1/4 and put olives on a ¼ of the pizza. Sprinkle the whole pizza lightly with cheese.

Veggie Pizza - Put red peppers on ¼ of the pizza, put olives on a ¼, put mushrooms on a ¼ and put green peppers on a ¼ of the pizza. Sprinkle the whole pizza lightly with cheese.

Hawaiian Pizza - Put ham on ¼ of the pizza, put pineapple on ¾ of the pizza. Sprinkle the whole pizza lightly with cheese.

Mighty Mushroom Pizza - Put mushrooms on ½ the pizza, onions on ¼ of the pizza and basil on ¼ of the pizza. Sprinkle the whole pizza lightly with cheese.

Year 1 English Lesson
Bee Lifecycle

Theme/Unit
Bees Knees

Lesson Overview
To begin to learn about the life of a bee.

Learning Objective
To write sentences, sequencing them to form a short narrative.

Success Criteria
Must: I know about the life cycle of the bee and that honey is sugar.
Should: I can name each phase.
Could: I can describe what happens at each phase

Introduction
Show the children a jar of honey and ask them what it is and where it comes from. Draw a picture of a bee on the WB/ show a picture, through questioning find out what they know about the bee and record key words in a thought shower e.g. insect, stripes, hive, sting, buzz, nectar, honey etc.

Explain that during this lesson they will be learning about the life cycle of the bee.

Main Teaching

Present the children with a large card circle divided into quarters and ask them what a life cycle is.

Consider the human life cycle e.g. baby, child, teenager and adult. Use the card circle to indicate each stage, the cyclical nature and discuss how we look different at each stage.

Refer back to the bee and key words. Pose the question: How might the life cycle of the bee begin? Explain the four stages of the life cycle of the bee (see Facts for the teacher).

Begin with laying the egg phase, draw an egg in a section on the card circle. Discuss this phase. Draw an arrow to the next section and question why the arrow. Continue, as above, with the larva, pupa and adult phases, discussing the features at each stage. Once the drawings are complete revisit the life cycle asking where would be a good place to start. Elicit a word/ label that best explains each phase e.g. egg, larva, pupa and adult. Model how to make some labels. Ask individual children to place them appropriately on the card circle.

Re-examine the life cycle a third time asking children for simple sentences to explain each stage. Model writing the sentences on strips of card. Encourage children to read them and place them beside the correct phase.

Finally jumble up the sentences and ask: Can you sort the sentences so they match up with the pictures? Read the sentences to form a short narrative.

Teacher Led and Independent Group Tasks

Make the life cycle of the bee and write about it. Show an example made earlier and talk through the steps. Choose a starting place on the plate. Draw the phase. Draw an arrow to the next phase. Draw that phase and so on.

(BA) Teaching assistant to work with the group to create their own the life cycle of the bee wheel on their plate. Begin identifying a starting place e.g. egg. Draw it carefully and discuss e.g. who laid it, where is it? Encourage them to draw a little arrow and continue on to the next phase similarly. When complete return to the beginning and elicit a suitable label for each phase e.g. egg, larva etc. Assist children labelling where necessary. Elicit a title and sentences. Encourage each child in the group to write a sentence, assisting when needed, sequencing the sentences to form a group narrative.

(A) To work quite independently, with teacher moving between the groups, to make their own life cycle of a bee wheel and label it. Encourage the children to work in pairs to make up a simple sentence to accompany each phase e.g. The queen bee lays an egg. Then write them quite independently (where necessary provide some sentences to read and to match up).

(HA) To work independently, making their own life cycle of the bee wheel, labelling it and generating their own sentence to accompany each picture. Aim to use 'and' in some of the sentences to join clauses e.g. The pupa hatches into an adult bee and chews its way out of the cell.

Plenary (AfL Focus)
Share life cycle wheels: consider labels; listen to each other's sentences; ask if a wheel is a good choice of equipment and why?

Revisit the learning objective and self-assess their learning using Steps to Success.

Ask them what else they would like to learn about the life of a bee and note.

Listen to The Flight of the Bumble Bee by Nikolai Rimsky-Korsakov.

Next Steps/Home Learning
English: Continue learning about the life of a bee: how bees make honey, how beekeepers harvest it.
Maths: Look at the shapes in the hive and tessellation.
Science: Visit some gardens or go online and look at bee hives.
D&T: Cooking and Nutrition: Learn to extract honey and use it to make different recipes.
Music: Listen to and learn about The Flight of the Bumble Bee (see web links).
Art and Design: Paint a bumblebee using your handprint.

Resources/Facts for the Teacher
Jar of honey, WB, coloured pens (black and yellow), picture of a bee (optional), large circle of card, labels, strips of card, large paper plates (one for each child).

Bees make the honeycomb in which the Queen Bee lays her eggs, with a waxy substance secreted from their tummies. The queen bee lays an egg in a cell of the honeycomb. The egg hatches into a larva (white and worm like).

The larva hatches into a pupa (shaped more like the bee, developing eyes, legs and wings). The pupa hatches into an adult bee and chews its way out of the cell. Bees have different roles: they can be queen bees, workers or drones.

The queens are the only female bees that produce eggs. The queen bee's role is to lay eggs. She lays about 2000 eggs a day. The drones mate with the new queens. They have no stinger. The worker bees collect food for the colony and feed the larvae. When a new queen bee is born, she either replaces a dying queen or leaves to start a colony of her own. A colony only has one queen bee.

Bees only sting when threatened and once they do sting they die. Bees also make honey which is a naturally unrefined sugar. To make a 500g of honey a colony of bees must collect nectar from approximately 2 million flowers and fly over 55,000 miles. In winter bees survive on honey which is very high in calories. They burn lots of calories keeping warm in cold winter months.

Children should eat a maximum of 6 teaspoons of sugar a day. So its important not to eat too much honey!

Year 1 History Lesson
Grow your Own (WW2)

Theme/Unit
Dig for Victory WW2

Lesson Overview
Children to learn how and why people planted and grew their own food during WW2.

Learning Objective
To find out how and why people in Britain grew their own food during WW2.

Success Criteria
Must: I know people grew their own food during WW2
Should: I know why they grew their own food.
Could: I can explain how people grew food.

Introduction
Visit the school garden, local garden or a local allotment. Look at the vegetable plot. Consider the shape and what vegetables are there. Return to class. Ask who grows food at home. Discuss.

Show the children a selection of 'Dig for Victory' posters on the IWB (see web links).

Have them consider the pictures and what message they are giving. Elicit the children's understanding of the word 'victory'.

Explain that in this lesson they will look at why and how people in Britain were asked to 'dig for victory' during World War 2.

Main Teaching

Tell the children that between 1939 and 1945 England was at war. Record on the WB: 1939 -1945.

Use a time line to help them understand how long ago it was.

Explain that while lots of people's lives changed during the war, e.g. people's safety, families being split up, men going off to war, the food shortage was a big problem for the Government. (see Facts for Teachers).

Record the government's problem as a question on the WB: How do we feed the people? Explain how they needed to act quickly to solve it so they began a 'Dig for Victory' Campaign, which they promoted using posters. Record the government's answer: 'Dig for Victory'. With this knowledge revisit some posters of the time and reconsider their message.

Explain/ elicit from the children:
- People were encouraged to grow their own food (posters). Consider the types of vegetables being grown in the pictures, e.g. potatoes, carrots, beetroots, cabbage, onions, runner beans, peas etc. Have a basket of vegetables at hand to show. Record the list on the WB as 'War Time Vegetables'.
- Children were expected to help by digging, planting and weeding (use photos).
- Women joined the Women's Land Army and took on all the farm work in the absence of the men.
- Dr Carrot and Potato Pete were cartoon characters introduced to appeal to children and encourage everyone to eat home grown vegetables (posters). Potatoes and carrots were easy to grow so were more plentiful and often used in place of less readily available ingredients so interesting recipes were written.

Teacher Led and Independent Group Tasks

Design a poster 'Dig for Victory'

(BA) Teaching Assistant to work with the group to assist them in designing an olden days' poster to encourage children/people to grow their own vegetables/ enjoy home grown vegetables during the war. Consider the posters they have already seen and what appealed. Elicit possible images and slogans. Question the group as to why people were encouraged to 'Dig for Victory' during WW2.

(A) Small groups to work with the gardener and helpers to prepare the soil and each plant a war time vegetable, e.g. runner beans, carrot seeds, lettuce and radish. Take photographs.

(HA) Teacher to work with this group to encourage them to design a 'Dig for Victory' poster with a message for us today. Consider the word 'victory' again and healthy eating. Listen to the children's ideas. Create a thought shower, e.g. eating more vegetables makes us healthier, freshly grown food is better quality, local food is cheaper, growing our own food saves on packaging etc. Children to work in pairs. Help each pair to decide on a picture and a message (slogan) before beginning.

Plenary (AfL Focus)

Encourage the children to share their learning: olden days 'Dig for Victory' posters, planting experience and modern 'Dig for Victory' posters. Discuss. Listen to Potato Pete's Song (see web links).

Revisit the learning objective and the success criteria and encourage the children to self-assess their learning.

Next Steps/Home Learning

Project in the town of Todmorden (people are encouraged to grow vegetables in unusual places including parks, station flowerbeds....)

D&T: Tend to the new plants in the vegetable patch.

D&T: Cooking and Nutrition: Make carrot fudge

Resources/Facts for the Teacher

IWB or Dig for Victory posters, Time Line, WB, a basket of war time vegetables preferably with leaves attached, e.g. carrots and beetroot, large sheets of paper per group, camera, plant seeds, child sized gardening tools, gloves and suitable clothing.

World War 2 (1939-1945): When Germany invaded Poland, Britain and France declared war on Germany. 1930's Britain imported 70 % of its food: 50% of its meat, 80% of its fruit, 70% of its cereals and 91% of its butter. Foodstuffs came from as far away as America and New Zealand by ship. However when the war started enemy submarines (U-boats) began sinking the ships hoping to starve the country into submission. In addition to this able-bodied men left farmland to fight and so farms were being neglected and producing less. The Ministry of Agriculture introduced the 'Dig for Victory' Campaign shortly after the war began. It wanted to make Britain as self-sufficient as possible with regards to feeding its people. It used posters, recipe books, visual recordings called 'food flashes' and popular songs to get its message across.

Everyone was encouraged to grow their own food, turn garden and flower beds into vegetable patches and mini allotments and rear chickens, rabbits, ducks and pigs in their gardens. Children were expected to help by digging, planting and weeding and some children worked as potato and fruit pickers on nearby farms (see web links).

Women joined the 'The Women's Land Army' and took on all the farm work in the absence of the men: they reared the animals; milked the cows; ploughed the fields; sowed the seeds and harvested the crops.

'Dr Carrot' and 'Potato Pete' were cartoon characters introduced to appeal to children and to encourage everyone to eat and enjoy homegrown vegetables. They appealed to popular culture of the time, had their own posters, songs and some nursery rhymes were adapted to fit their cause. Potatoes and carrots were easy to grow so were plentiful and filling. They were often used in place of less readily available ingredients. Consequently advice on how to best prepare them, e.g. scrubbing instead of peeling helps reduce waste, and new recipes showing how to use the vegetables in interesting ways were suggested, e.g. carrot jam, carrot fudge and even toffee carrots.

Carrot recipes (see web links).

Gardening Guides for Children (see web links).

Year 1 Art & Design Lesson
Fruit and Vegetable Portraits

Theme/Unit
Food Printing

Lesson Overview
To begin to explore mark making, inspired by Giuseppe Arcimboldo, an Italian artist who created portraits using fruit and vegetables.

Learning Objective
To select fruit and vegetables for their shape and colour in order to create portraits, using a variety of tools.

Success Criteria
Must: I can identify fruit and vegetables.
Should: I can create a portrait selecting fruit and vegetables for their shape and colour.
Could: I can use an art vocabulary to describe the visual properties of the fruit and vegetables.

Introduction
Through questioning examine a basket of fruit and vegetables.
What are their names?
Are they fruit or vegetables?
What colour are they?
What do they look like?
How do they feel?
What do they smell like?
Have you ever tasted them?

Introduce a picture of Giuseppe Arcimboldo, an Italian painter who lived a long time ago, who created very imaginative portraits.

Ask the children what they think a portrait is.

Main Teaching

Show the children some examples of Giuseppe Arcimboldo's paintings on the IWB (see web links).

Explain that they are paintings. Study them. Elicit what the children see. Encourage them to look more closely at the features on the faces and notice the different fruits and vegetables Arcimboldo has used, e.g. the cheeks are made of apples, the nose is a pear, the eye brows etc. Discuss e.g. can they explain why Giuseppe has used apples for cheeks? Model using an art vocabulary e.g. they are curved, shiny, rosy coloured.

Have the children sit in pairs to study each other's features, e.g. noses, cheeks, eyes, eyebrows, eyelashes etc. Ask if they can they imagine any fruit or vegetables that would best create these. Listen to their suggestions and ask if they can justify them, e.g. olives are round, black and shiny like pupils of the eyes or broccoli is curly looking like hair.

Tell the children that they will be creating portraits using fruit and vegetables. Model making some examples using the children's suggestions, e.g. apple segments for lips, olives for eyes, peas in pods for eyebrows, broccoli for hair etc.

Demonstrate cutting the fruit/vegetables using a knife showing the children the bridge knife technique and the claw knife technique. Explain how there will be set cutting stations in the classroom that are supervised by adults and that is where the knives and scissors will be if needed. Reinforce the importance of using knives and scissors safely.

Show a child's portrait interpretation (see web links).

Teacher Led and Independent Group Tasks

Children to work in mixed ability groups to create a fruit and vegetable group portrait, inspired by Giuseppe Arcimboldo, using supervised cutting techniques.

Provide each group with a basket of fruit and vegetables with which to work. Remind the children to consider what fruit and vegetables they will use for the different features of the face. Encourage discussion using words to describe the fruit and vegetables' visual characteristics – form, colour and texture.

Reiterate how to use the cutting stations safely, and only with adult supervision.

Teaching Assistant and parent helpers to supervise the cutting stations. Teacher to work between the groups, questioning and advising where necessary. Take photographs of the finished portraits.

Plenary (AfL Focus)

Encourage the children to 'take a walk' around the classroom and admire their friends' fruit and vegetable portraits. Once assembled on the carpet, congratulate them all on their creations, look at the photographs and allow them to evaluate what they've seen, e.g. Who used the grapes in a clever way? What vegetable was good to use for hair?

Explain that next session they will be using their new ideas to print portraits using cut fruit and vegetables. Demonstrate how to press print using fruit and vegetables. Show an inked tray, a roller, some cut fruit/

vegetables and cartridge paper. Using the roller ink-block the fruit/vegetable (note less ink is better), press the fruit/vegetable onto the paper, lift it directly up (to ensure clear definition). Consider the print.

Show the children some examples of fruit and vegetable print portraits you made earlier to inspire them and encourage them to think about their designs for next time.

Revisit the learning objective and self-assess their learning using Steps to Success.

Next Steps/Home Learning
Art & Design: Use the fruit and vegetable portraits to inspire the children to print their own portraits using cut fruit and vegetables.

Home Learning: Look more closely at fruit and vegetables at home, their shapes and textures. Think, like Giuseppe Arcimboldo, about how you could use them to print a portrait.

Resources/Facts for the Teacher:
A basket of fruit and vegetables to examine, IWB, enough baskets of fruit and vegetables to have one per working group (lemons, celery, apples, carrots, onions, mushrooms, corn on the cob, peas in pods/mange tout, grapes, peppers, courgettes, potatoes, broccoli, cauliflower, tomatoes, olives), camera, knives and scissors, chopping boards, printing ink, ink tray, roller, cartridge paper.

Giuseppe Arcimboldo (1527-1593), was an Italian artist who painted imaginative portrait heads made entirely from fruit, vegetables, books and fish.

Cutting techniques (see web links):
Cutting food with scissors e.g. apricots, dates

Bridge knife technique with soft foods
e.g. strawberry, olive

Bridge knife technique with hard food
e.g. apple

Claw knife technique with soft food
e.g. courgette

Claw knife technique with hard food
e.g. carrot

Simple combination of bridge and claw
e.g. onion

Year 2 Lesson Overview

Subject	Learning Objectives	Curriculum Links	Cross Curricular Links	Page Numbers
Maths Rocket Lollies	To measure accurately using ml.	**Ma2/2.1:** Number and Place Value Ma2/2.1a: Count in steps of 2, 3, and 5 from 0, and in tens from any number, forward and backward **Ma2/2.2:** Addition & Subtraction Ma2/2.2a: Solve problems with addition and subtraction: using concrete objects and pictorial representations, including those involving numbers, quantities and measures **Ma2/3.1: Measurement** Ma2/3.1a: Choose and use appropriate standard units to estimate and measure length/height in any direction (m/cm); mass (kg/g); temperature (°C); capacity (litres/ml) to the nearest appropriate unit, using rulers, scales, thermometers and measuring vessels	English, Science, History, D&T: Cooking and Nutrition	50, 51, 52

Subject	Learning Objectives	Curriculum Links	Cross Curricular Links	Page Numbers
Science Food Sources	To identify sources of food (Living Things).	**Sc2/1 Working Scientifically** Sc2/1 Identifying and classifying Sc2/2.3 Animals including humans Sc2/2.3c Describe the importance for humans of exercise, eating the right amounts of different types of food, and hygiene.	Geography, D&T: Cooking and Nutrition	53, 54, 55
History The Great Fire Diary	To plan a diary entry.	Hi1/1.2 Events beyond living memory that are significant nationally or globally	Maths, English, Science, D&T: Cooking and Nutrition	56, 57, 58
RE Hot Cross Buns	To make a hot cross bun.	Religious Festivals – Christianity: Easter	Maths, D&T: Cooking and Nutrition	59, 60, 61

Year 2 Maths Lesson
Rocket Lollies

Theme/Unit
Great Explorers/ Neil Armstrong.

Lesson Overview
Children to use millilitres to make frozen rocket lollies.

Learning Objective
To measure accurately using ml.

Success Criteria
Must: I know to use millilitres when measuring capacity.
Should: I can measure accurately in millilitres.
Could: I can solve simple problems using millilitres

Introduction
Using a counting stick practise counting on together in 2s, 5s and 10s.

Vary the starting place, count on and back and change direction.

Ask individual children to begin and others to continue.

Extend the learning by encouraging the children to use their tables to continue but count on in 20s, 50s and 100s.

Main Teaching

Briefly refer to Neil Armstrong, his moon landing in Apollo 11 and how he and Buzz Aldrin were on the moon for over 21 hours. Comment on how amazing the rocket must have been to travel to the moon, gauge the distance and the speed, record the temperature and the amount of fuel used etc.

Ask the children what they think they might have been doing during their time there (guide them towards measuring). Discuss.

Present the children with a selection of measuring equipment e.g. tape measure, weighing scales, calendar, clock, thermometer, measuring jug etc. Question to find out what they know: What is the equipment? What unit of measure does it use?

Explain that this lesson they will focus on capacity: reading scales on measuring jugs using millilitres.

Show some containers and a litre measuring jug on the IWB. Read the scale on the litre(l) measuring jug. Count together in 100s. Discuss 1000ml = 1 litre. Encourage the children to estimate how many ml each container might contain. Tip the contents of the various containers into the litre jug. Practise reading the scales.

Next display a selection of measuring jugs, some ml amounts on cards and some water. Ask selected children to pour the given amount of water into each jug. Have other children check the results and where necessary correct.

Finally look at a 100ml container on the IWB and how it might be filled using one colour, read the scale. Suggest two children work together to fill the container to 100ml, each pouring in the same amount.

Can they explain how they work it out? (Model 50ml+50ml =100ml) Similarly with three children (30ml+30ml+30ml r. 10ml) and then with five (20ml+20ml+20ml+20ml+20ml).
Model pictures. What do they notice?

Teacher Led and Independent Group Tasks

Explain to the children that as an activity they will use their measuring skills to make rocket ice lollies. Show the rocket ice lolly moulds which each hold 100ml and the different coloured/flavoured fruit and vegetable juices available to choose from. Debate the health benefits to regular ice lollies.

(BA) Teaching Assistant to work with group to make some rocket ice lollies. Initially ask how they would make a one juice flavoured lolly: What flavour? How many ml would you need? Where is 100ml on the measuring jug? Once competent, children to make the lollies: Pour juice into the jug. Check it is the correct amount. Pour juice into the mould. Freeze. Ask can they make a rocket ice lolly using equal amounts of two fruit/vegetable juices? Encourage them to read the scale on the litre jug and to use their number bonds to 10 to help them work out how much of each juice they need. Ensure they know that 50ml +50ml =100ml. Children to record two-coloured lollies in pictures on individual WBs.

(A) As above, working with a partner, ask the children to make a two-coloured rocket lolly using the same amount of each juice and then a five—coloured lolly. Record on WBs

(HA) Teacher to work with the group to facilitate them making a three-coloured lolly. Discuss remainders. Then encourage them to work more independently to make a five-coloured lolly, as above, while the teacher moves among the other groups. Record on WBs.

Plenary (AfL Focus)
Begin counting brusquely in 10's, 20s, 50s and 30's
to 100. What do they notice?

Ask individual children to show their lolly drawings e.g.
a two-coloured lolly. Encourage them to talk about the
flavours and explain how they measured them equally.
Elicit 50ml +50ml=100ml and 'millilitres'. Engage the
others by asking how else the lolly could look using the
same colours e.g. a red base and green top or green
base and red top. Are there any other possibilities?
Continue as above examining three-coloured lolly
examples and five—coloured lolly examples.

Extension: Each time check the various possibilities/
colour combinations. Record on the WB.

Revisit the learning objective and self-assess their
learning using Steps to Success.

Next Steps/Home Learning
D&T: Evaluate the frozen lollies and enjoy them.
Science: Consider how liquids expand when frozen and
whether or not it would be wise to leave a 5ml gap at the
top of the mould to allow for this.

Resources/Facts for the Teacher
Counting sticks, a selection of measuring equipment:
tape measure, weighing scales, calendar, clock, ruler,
thermometer, measuring jug etc. IWB, several measuring
jugs with clear markings to 100ml, cards marked
with 20ml, 50ml, 30ml, water, a selection of fruit and
vegetable juices, rockets ice lolly moulds and individual
WBs and pens.

Year 2 Science Lesson
Food Sources

Theme/Unit
Living Things, animals including humans.

Lesson Overview
To explore where our food comes from.

Learning Objective
To identify sources of food.

Success Criteria
Must: I know that all foods come from plants and animals.
Should: I know where my food comes from.
Could: I can sort foods into groups according to their source.

Introduction
Begin questioning the children to establish what they already know. What did you eat for breakfast/lunch today? Why do we eat? What would happen if we didn't eat?

Establish that food is very important for us but its important to eat a balance diet with lots of food groups.

Explain that in this lesson we will be looking at where our food comes from and the effects that too much food can have on our bodies.

Main Teaching

Present the children with a basket of food stuffs that typify food from other countries e.g. pasta, curry, noodles, rice etc. Ask where they come from, have they tasted any, and label accordingly.

Next show a basket of food stuffs/pictures that someone would buy at the supermarket e.g. cereal, peas, eggs, bacon, bananas, butter, honey, fish fingers, pasta, yogurt, bread, biscuits etc. and arrange them into two sets. Elicit how each set should be labelled (From Plants and From Animals) and why.

Show the children some foods which are very high in sugar eg cereal, biscuits, cake and then compare to some fruit. Explain that fruit has natural sugar in it and the other foods have refined sugar. Tell the children its very important not to eat more than 6 teaspoons of sugar a day.

Finally present a basket of food with a selection of animal produce as above but more fruit and vegetables including root and leafy (some fruit and vegetables from source with soil and leaves on). Ask volunteers to sort the selection into sets and explain why e.g. fruit, vegetables, meat or from animals, from under the ground, from trees, from plants. Discuss and label accordingly.

Add a cucumber, squash or tomatoes which all have seeds. Discuss which part of the plant we eat. Establish that fruits have seeds and grow on plants, bushes and trees, while vegetables can be root vegetables, leafy vegetables or other (see Facts for Teachers) and meat and other produce comes from animals.

Ask some children what their favourite meals are and together decide where the foods came from e.g. spaghetti bolognaise – mince from animals, tomato sauce from plants, spaghetti from plants and cheese from animals.

Teacher Led and Independent Group Tasks

Design a 'Where does it come from?' board game. (See web links about 'From Farm to Fork!').

(BA) Teaching Assistant to work with the group to design and make a simple board game for the group to play, entitled 'Where does it come from?' e.g. design a board with two sets/baskets/plates labelled 'From Plants' and 'From Animals'. Have the children each make 6 game cards with a food on each e.g. yogurt, raisins, toast, eggs etc. Ensure they do not repeat any. Remind them of the name of the game. Discuss the rules e.g. shuffle the cards, deal them so each player has 6 cards, take turns to place each card in the correct set.

(A) Work in small groups to play a pre-prepared game (see web links 'From Farm to Fork!'). Encourage the children to read through the rules and think about their choices.

(HA) Work as a group, with the Teacher, to design and make a 'Where does it come from?' board game for the group to play. Establish what needs doing e.g. designing and making the board, making 'food cards', making 'where does it come from cards' and agreeing on the rules. Suggest they consider where the food comes from to include trees, bushes, root and leafy vegetable categories.

Plenary (AfL Focus)

Share game ideas and allow some time
to play each other's games. Ask if the games help
us to understand where our food comes from.

Watch a Field to Fork film (see web links).

Revisit the learning objective and self-assess their
learning using Steps to Success.

Next Steps/Home Learning

English: Read Oliver's Vegetables by Vivian French.
Science: Explore the different food groups and
understand why we need to eat a balanced diet.
D&T: Cooking and Nutrition: Choose a food, source it and
make a meal.
Home Learning: When eating think about where your
meal comes from. When visiting the supermarket
consider the differences between fruit and vegetables
at source and when packaged.

Resources/Facts for the Teacher

Three baskets of food as above, sets rings and labels,
print and prepare copies of the 'From Farm to Fork!'
board game (see web links), several large sheets of card,
small game cards.

A fruit is the part of the plant that contains seeds e.g.
apple, pear, kiwi and lemon. It is usually soft and juicy
but may have a tough outer layer e.g. melon. Some fruits
grow on trees e.g. oranges, lemons, coconuts, peaches
and plums. Some fruits grow on vines e.g. watermelon
grow on vines near the ground while grapes grow on
vines that climb. Other fruits grow on bushes e.g.
strawberries, raspberries and blueberries.

The pineapple grows on a plant near the ground.
Tomatoes, pumpkin, avocado and cucumber are all fruits
because they have seeds.

Vegetables come from many different parts of the plant:
the root, the leaves, the flowers, the stems and seeds.
Root vegetables grow under the ground e.g. potatoes,
carrots, beetroot and turnips. Leafy vegetables grow
above the ground e.g. lettuce, cabbage and spinach.
When we eat broccoli and cauliflower we eat the flower
buds, that haven't yet opened. We eat the stem of the
asparagus and celery. When we eat corn or peas we are
eating the seeds of the plant.

Sugar is often 'hidden' in processed foods e.g. baked
beans. Explain to the children that it's important not to
eat too much sugar and it should be viewed as a treat.

Year 2 History Lesson
The Great Fire Diary

Theme/Unit
The Great Fire of London

Lesson Overview
To understand how The Great Fire
of London started.

Previous Learning
Begin to learn about The Great Fire of
London with Magic Grandad who takes
the children back in time to meet Samuel
Pepys. Focus on his writing of a diary
and consider the properties of a diary.
As a class write an excerpt from Samuel
Pepys' diary.

Learning Objective
To plan a diary entry.

Success Criteria
Must: I know how The Great Fire
of London started.
Should: I understand the role
of Mr Farriner.
Could: I can explain what happened.

Introduction
Revisit through questioning what the
children already know about the Great
Fire of London.

Ask what else they want to find out and
guide them towards such questions as:
Where did it start?
Who started it?
How did it start?
How long did it last?
How did they stop it?

Choose the question 'How did it start?'
as the focus for the lesson.

Main Teaching

Introduce Thomas Farriner, as a baker, who lived in Pudding Lane in London in 1666. Discuss the role of a baker: bakery, making bread, ovens, long days, early starts...

Model making bread. Consider the ingredients needed and elicit the appropriate vocabulary to explain how to make bread. Have a child act as a scribe to record the words in a class word bank on the WB e.g. flour, salt, yeast, mix, knead.

Suggest each child 'go back in time' and pretend they are Thomas Farriner, the baker. Give them each a portion of dough to handle, knead and shape. Elicit how it feels and smells. Add words to the class word bank e.g. smooth, sticky, tacky...

Show a picture of an oven then and explain how it worked, talking through how to light it, heat it and bake bread in it (see web links).

Briefly compare to modern ovens and explain how The Great Fire of London started with a fire in an oven (see Facts for Teachers).

Encourage the children to think briefly about what they already know to explain why the fire spread so quickly.

Teacher Led and Independent Group Tasks

You are Thomas Farriner, can you explain how the fire started?

(BA) Role Play Task: Teaching Assistant to lead the group giving them the opportunity to re-enact what Thomas Farriner, the baker, might have done towards starting the fire e.g. the day before he mixed ingredients (include descriptions about kneading and textures using words from the class word bank), lit the oven, baked the bread, tidied up for the day... Discuss.

Oral task: Encourage each child, as Mr. Farriner, to recount how the fire started? (Ensure they use the first person, past tense, chronological order, time onnectives, a variety of action verbs to make it interesting.), Listen to each other.

Teaching Assistant to make some group notes for a diary entry.

(A) and (HA) Tasks as above but children to work in pairs and take turns, beginning with role play and progressing to recounts. Remind the children to use the first person, past tense, time connectives and a variety of action verbs to make their retelling of how the fire started interesting. Teacher to assist where necessary.

Children to each record some notes to help with their diary entry for next time.

Plenary (AfL Focus)

Share experiences. Have some children re-enact how the fire started, others to recount the story as Thomas Farriner and some to share their notes.

Revisit the learning objective and self-assess their learning using Steps to Success.

Finish by singing London's Burning as a round.

Next Steps/Home Learning

D&T: Cooking and Nutrition: Bake the bread rolls.
English: Pretend you are Mr Farriner, the baker.
Use your word bank and notes to write in your diary what happened on the day the fire started. Begin 'Dear Diary...'

Home Learning: Find out more about The Great Fire of London online by playing a Fire of London game (see web links).

Resources/Facts for the Teacher

Bread making resources: flour, salt, yeast, mixing bowl, weighing scales, clean surfaces. IWB.

The Great Fire started in Pudding Lane on Sunday, September 2nd, 1666. Thomas Farriner, a baker, forgot to put out the fire in an oven at the end of a day's work. A spark flew from the oven and landed on some nearby kindling. It smouldered and caught fire. It set the whole bake house on fire.

The fire spread quickly because the summer in London had been very dry, an easterly wind was blowing, houses were mostly made of timber and there was no fire brigade or easy access to water other than by the river.

Year 2 RE Lesson
Hot Cross Buns

Theme/Unit
Symbols of Easter

Lesson Overview
To explore the link between Christian beliefs and the symbolic meaning behind the hot cross

Learning Objective
To understand why hot cross buns are symbolic to Christians.

Success Criteria
Must: I know what symbols are.
Should: I know why the hot cross bun is symbolic.
Could: I understand why symbols are important.

Introduction
Show the class some examples of common symbols e.g. Superman, a road sign and toilet sign

Ask what they mean/ what they make them think about. Ask what love and happiness are and how they might be represented in symbols. Listen to their suggestions. Elicit other examples.

Explain that 'symbols' are pictures or objects that tell us something or make us think of something. They represent something.

During this lesson they are going to learn about a symbol that is important to Christians.

Main Teaching

Present the children with a cross. Ask what it makes them think of. Discuss.
Refer to/read the Easter story.

Establish that Jesus died on a cross.
The cross reminds Christians that God loved them so much that he sent his only son. Many Christians feel that symbols help them concentrate on God when they pray.

Ask the children what reminds them of Easter e.g. Easter eggs, Easter bunny, Easter bonnets, Easter egg hunts etc.
Can they explain why?

Show some hot cross buns.
Ask: Who likes them? How do you like to eat them? Can you see the cross?

Explain that they are usually eaten at Easter and reiterate that they are symbolic because Jesus died on the cross and the cross reminds Christians that God loved them so much that he sent his only son to Earth.

Teacher Led and Independent Group Tasks

Make hot cross buns.

Children to work individually or in pairs to make their own hot cross buns.

Focus on Cooking and Nutrition Skills: weighing, measuring, rubbing butter into flour, beating, dividing mixture, forming dough, shaping and glazing.

Discuss yeast and the fermentation process.

Plenary (AfL Focus)

Sing 'Hot Cross Buns'. While waiting for the hot cross buns to bake watch a short 'Celebrating Easter' film and/or how yeast helps bread to rise (see web links).

Revisit the learning objective and self-assess their learning using Steps to Success.

Next Steps/Home Learning

Maths: Explore shape and fractions (1/4).
Home Learning: Make the buns at home. Try some variety such as apple and cinnamon or wholewheat.

Resources/Facts for the Teacher

Pictures of symbols, a cross, the Easter story, some hot cross buns.

Cooking Equipment: Access to ovens, baking sheets, saucepans, small bowl/cup (egg), mixing bowls, wooden spoons, measuring jugs, scales, tablespoons, teaspoons, piping bags/freezer bas, scissors, glazing brush.

Yeast: As the yeast eat the sugar, a process called anaerobic fermentation begins to take place. The by-products of this process are alcohol and carbon dioxide. During this time, the carbon dioxide is trapped by a series of strands of gluten (in the flour), which allows the dough to rise.

Hot Cross Bun Recipe

Ingredients
250g strong white bread
flour (can use gluten-free)
¼ tsp. salt
2 tsp. mixed spice
25g caster sugar
25g butter, soft
100g mixed dried fruit
3.5g dried-yeast
100 ml milk
1 egg, beaten
Crosses and glaze:
2 tbsp. plain flour
Honey, for brushing

Method
1. Combine the flour, salt, sugar and mixed spice.
2. Rub in the butter with your fingertips. Stir in the fruit and yeast.
3. Gently warm the milk (not too hot) and beat in the egg then pour onto the dry ingredients.
4. Mix ingredients together to form dough. Cut up into 4 equal pieces (you can weigh to check too).
5. Flour the tabletop and shape the dough into buns. Space them out on a baking sheet and cover with cling film. Leave in a warm place for an hour when they should have grown in size.
6. Heat the oven to 200C°/Gas mark 7. Mix the plain flour with 1 tbsp. to make a paste. Pour into a piping bag/ freezer bag and pipe a cross onto each bun.
7. Bake for 12-15 minutes until risen and golden. Brush with honey to glaze and enjoy.

Year 3 Lessons

Maths
English
Geography
History

Year 3 Lesson Overview

Subject	Learning Objectives	Curriculum Links	Cross Curricular Links	Page Numbers
Maths Vending Machine	To solve 2-step word problems using money.	**Ma3/2.3: Multiplication & Division** Ma3/2.3a: recall and use multiplication and division facts for the 3, 4 and 8 multiplication tables Ma3/2.3b: write and calculate mathematical statements for multiplication using the multiplication tables that they know Ma3/2.3c: Solve problems involving multiplication **Ma3/3.1: Measurement** Ma3/3.1c: add and subtract amounts of money to give change, using both £ and p in practical contexts	D&T: Cooking and Nutrition	66, 67, 68
English Food Alliteration	To write and recite a verse using alliteration.	**En3/1 Spoken Language**: En3/1c use relevant strategies to build their vocabulary En3/1i participate in discussions, presentations, performances, roleplay/improvisations and debates **En3/2.2 Comprehension** En3/2.2a develop positive attitudes to reading, and an understanding of what they read, by vii discussing words and phrases that capture the reader's interest and imagination viii recognising some different forms of poetry **En3/3.3 Composition** En3/3.3a Plan their writing by: i. discussing writing similar to that which they are planning to write in order to understand and learn from its structure, vocabulary and grammar ii. discussing and recording ideas En3/3.3b Draft and write by: i. composing and rehearsing sentences orally . ii. En3/3.3e read their own writing aloud, to a group or the whole class, using appropriate intonation and controlling the tone and volume so that the meaning is clear.	D&T: Cooking and Nutrition	69, 70, 71

Subject	Learning Objectives	Curriculum Links	Cross Curricular Links	Page Numbers
Geography Create a starter	To learn about foods typical of Italy.	**Ge2/1.1 Locational Knowledge** Ge2/1.1a locate the world's countries, using maps to focus on Europe (including the location of Russia) and North and South America, concentrating on their environmental regions, key physical and human characteristics, countries, and major cities **Ge2/1.3 Human and Physical Geography** Ge2/1.3a describe and understand key aspects of physical geography, including: climate zones, biomes and vegetation belts, rivers, mountains, volcanoes and earthquakes, and the water cycle Ge2/1.3b describe and understand key aspects of human geography, including: types of settlement and land use, economic activity including trade links, and the distribution of natural resources including energy, food, minerals and water	D&T: Cooking and Nutrition, Art, ICT	72, 73, 74
History Afternoon Tea	To learn about the history of afternoon tea, a food tradition that is still popular today.	— The changing power of monarchs using case studies such as John, Anne and Victoria — Changes in an aspect of social history, such as crime and punishment from the Anglo-Saxons to the present or leisure and entertainment in the 20th Century — A study of an aspect or theme in British history that extends pupils' chronological knowledge beyond 1066	D&T: Cooking and Nutrition, Art, ICT	75, 76, 77

Year 3 Maths Lesson
Vending Machine

Theme/Unit
Money

Lesson Overview
Children to design a vending machine multiplication game using a fruit box, dividers and fruit.

Learning Objective
To solve 2-step word problems using money.

Success Criteria
Must: I can solve 2-step word problems.
Should: I use my times tables to solve the problems.
Could: I can find change.

Introduction
Missing Numbers/ Complete the Pattern. Children to complete independently on WBs using given sequences of multiples from x2, x5, x10, x3, x4 and x8 tables, as displayed on IWB.

Tell the children that you need their help to design a vending machine. Who has used a vending machine? Share their experiences. Discuss the usual contents and how healthy they are.

Explain that you want to create a multiplication game about healthy snacks called 'The Vending Machine'. While ideally it would be online it seems best to make it first.

Main Teaching

Show a fruit box with dividers, ask for ideas e.g. what healthy snacks would they include. Reiterate the challenge to design a multiplication game. Ellicit how best to do this e.g. arrange the snacks in rows/ arrays and decide on how much each snack would cost and assign price tags. Using the box, dividers and snacks model this with their help.

Encourage them to make up simple multiplication problems to solve e.g. How much will I spend if I buy 2 apples?

Can they write the simple number sentences on their WBs?

Introduce the idea of getting change e.g. If I have 20p and I buy two apples how much change will I get? Elicit how there were 2 steps to solving the problem. What are they? Can they record each step? Step1. 2x5p=10p, Step 2. 20p -10p=10p

Continue as above with their problems. Record an example of a problem and the number sentence on the class white board and establish as the game's Easy Level.

Explain how many online games have different levels. If those problems were the easy level, ask how they could make them a little bit trickier so they are a medium level and still have 2 steps e.g. How much will I spend if I buy two apples and some grapes? What are the 2 steps? Can they record? Step1. 2x10p=20p, Step2. 20p + 4p=24p. Suggest the prices could be based on x2, x3, x4 and x5 tables. Agree on level of difficulty and record as above

under Medium Level.
Continue prompting problems for the hard level e.g. If I buy 2 apples, some grapes and a carton of milk how much change will I have from 50p/ £1.00. Discuss: Are there more than 2 steps to the problem? What are they? Can you do some in your head? How would you record it? Listen to suggestions. Suggest basing price tags on x3, x4, x5 and x8 tables. Agree on the level of difficulty and record examples on the whiteboard under Hard Level.

Teacher Led and Independent Group Tasks

(BA) Teaching Assistant to work with group to make a vending machine of healthy snacks, agree prices based on x2, x3 x5 and x10 tables and make price tags. Together formulate 2-step word problems orally based on the Easy Level example on IWB. TA to record word problems. Children to talk through 2-step process together and record number sentences independently, using coins where necessary.

(A) As above but in pairs, using the vending machine created earlier in the lesson, with price tags based on x2, x3, x4 and x5. Children to work through some pre prepared 2-step word problems for the medium level e.g. How much will I spend if I buy two apples and some grapes?

Extension

To create and record 2—step word problems of their own.

(HA) Teacher to work with group to make a vending machine of healthy snacks, agree prices based on x3, x4, x5 and x8 tables and make price tags. With Teacher leading initially, children to formulate word

problems orally based on the Hard Level example on
IWB. Consider the number of steps involved and how
necessary it is to record each step.

Extension
Once confident, children to generate, solve and record
their own word problems independently.

Plenary (AfL Focus)
Ask each group to display their vending machine and set
some word problems for the class to solve.

Question the children on how they solve the problems.

Revisit the learning objective and self assess their
learning using Steps to Success.

Next Steps/Home Learning
Maths: Send some children from (BA) group to Year 2
with their vending machine to explain what they have
been learning and try it out with the younger children.

Similarly send some children from (HA) to Year 4.

Keep (A) group's vending machine in class and display
with coin trays for their own use during choosing time.

Resources/Facts for the Teacher
IWB and individual WBs and pens, several fruit boxes
with dividers, selection of healthy snacks, price tags, coin
trays and pre-prepared medium level word problems.

Year 3 English Lesson
Food Alliteration

Theme/Unit

Lesson Overview
To write and recite a verse using alliteration.

Learning Objective
To write and recite a verse using alliteration.

Success Criteria
Must: I know what alliteration is.
Should: I can write and recite simple verses using alliteration.
Could: I understand and can explain why alliteration is used.

Introduction
Explain briefly how food is an important part of life even from when we are very young. Very often singing or chanting about food helps us to learn about it and appreciate it. Encourage the children to share their food related rhymes and simple poems about food from home, e.g. I Eat My Peas with Honey, Five Fat Sausages etc.

Discuss. Do they always rhyme? Do they have a rhythm? Do some words/lines repeat?

Main Teaching

Present the tongue twister Betty Botter Bought Some Butter on the IWB. Have fun trying to say it in unison. Discuss. Draw attention to the repeating initial sounds. Elicit Betty Botter bought ... butter as alliteration. Explain. Ask the pupils to find other examples in the verse.

Examine the structure of the sentence Betty Botter bought some butter. Can the children identify the noun? Can they identify the verb? Where might you add an adjective in the sentence?

Model some examples on the WB: Alfie Adams bought some ...   Curly Chloe bought some ... Quick fire question the use of nouns, proper nouns, adjectives and verbs.

Mini activity: If Alfie Adams bought some apples, Betty Botter bought some butter and Curly Chloe bought some cabbage what might the other letters of the alphabet buy? Assign a letter of the alphabet and encourage Talking Pairs to make up a sentence using alliteration e.g. Dizzy Daisy bought some dumplings. Freddy Farrow bought some fish. Listen to each other's ideas.

Extension:

Elicit how we might improve on these simple sentences e.g. think of verbs that fit the pattern. Can children improve on their simple sentence incorporating a verb to fit e.g. Alfie Adams ate some apples, Chloe Curly cut some cabbage, Dizzy Daisy dunked some doughnuts.

Teacher Led and Independent Group Tasks

(BA) Teacher to work with group to create a group verse using Betty Botter bought some butter as a framework. Encourage each child to create a line orally using their own name to determine the pattern of alliteration e.g. Mini Maggie munched on muffins. Share ideas. Write on whiteboards, support with spelling strategies. Together order the sentences to build into a group verse. Children to record group verse using a writing framework.

(A) Teaching Assistant to work with the group to help them create word lists:

Adjective	Noun	Verb	Noun (food)
Curly	Alfie Adams Betty Botter Chloe	ate bought chomped	apples butter couscous

Children can use the word lists to explore and create simple food verses independently using alliteration. Record verses.

(HA) As above but in pairs, group to create Acrostic Poem of your school name, e.g. Charlton Manor using initial letters to determine alliteration.

Plenary (AfL Focus)
Share verses. Discuss alliteration. Revisit the learning objective and self assess their learning using Steps to Success.

Next Steps/Home Learning
English: Edit and best copy verses.
Home Learning: Suggest children share some verses with their family before or after mealtimes.

Resources/Facts for the Teacher
A selection of food related nursery rhymes, Betty Botter Bought Some Butter by Carolyn Wells.

Adjectives describe a noun Alliteration is the repetition of the same sound or letter at the beginning of each or most of the words in a sentence. Nouns are people, places or things. Proper Nouns name a specific person, place or thing. Verbs are action or 'doing words'.

Tongue Twisters are phrases or sentences that are tricky to say.

Year 3 Geography Lesson
Create a Starter

Theme/Unit

Lesson Overview
Create a whole class Italian Recipe Book.

Learning Objective
To learn about foods typical of Italy.

Success Criteria
Must: I know what foods come from Italy.
Should: I know where Italy is in the world.
Could: I know how olive oil is made.

Introduction
Present the children with some bags of shopping and examine the contents together. Briefly consider the variety of different foodstuffs. Ask individual children to sort the items into sets and encourage the others to work out the reason why. (Be mindful that ideally you want someone to sort in countries of origin so guide accordingly.)

Once the foodstuffs are sorted, look at a world map.

Question the children to establish what they already know: Can you find the countries of origin? Where in the world are they? What else do you know about the country? Have you ever visited? Can you name an important city there?

Explain how today we are learning about Italy. Show a map and use prepared Fact Cards to share some/all of the following facts.

— The flag of Italy is a green, white, and red vertical tricolor. What is a tricolor
— Italy lies in Southern Europe. How long do you think a flight from London to Rome would take? (Roughly 2.5 hours).
— Italy is easy to recognize on any world map. Can you see why? The country is shaped like a high-heeled boot. It looks like the boot is kicking a ball, which is the island of Sicily
— In the North, the mountain range of the Alps separates Italy from the other European countries. Use the map to help you name them. (France, Switzerland, Austria and Slovenia.)

— In the South of Italy you will find Italy's three active volcanoes: Vesuvius near Naples, Etna on Sicily and Stromboli off the Coast of Italy.
— Terrain is mostly rugged and mountainous (Alps and Apennine mountains) with some plains and coastal lowlands. Locate on map.
— Climate is predominantly Mediterranean; Alpine in far north; hot and dry in south.

Show some typical Italian foods, elicit their names and discuss: Pizza, Calzone, Pasta, Lasagne, Spaghetti bolognaise, Pasta and Pesto, Tomato and Mozzarella salad, Antipasti, Olive Oil and bread.

Main Teaching

Explain to the children that as a class they are going to make an Italian recipe book. Today's task is to plan a starter. Talk about what a starter is, when it is eaten, what size it is.

Show possible plate sizes, bowls and ingredients. Refer back to the typical Italian foods e.g. salads, antipasti, pasta and dough based. Consider the combinations. Suggest they work as a group and follow the given steps. Display the steps and talk through them.

1. Smell and taste the samples. Consider the colours and textures of each of the foods. Record group likes and dislikes simply e.g. tally chart.
2. Think and talk about combining two or three of the foods to make a tasty
and attractive looking starter. Agree on ingredients.
3. Talk through the design. Agree on a plate size. Record what the starter will look like (labelled diagram).
4. Create a shopping list in preparation for the next lesson.

Teacher Led and Independent Group Tasks

Children to work through the steps in mixed ability groups, Teacher and TA to work between the groups, differentiation by outcome.

Extension

Use the Internet to search 'how olive oil is made' and watch a short film (see web links).

Plenary (AfL Focus)

Each group to tell the class about their starter, showing the labelled diagram and naming the ingredients. Invite other children to comment on the presentation, portion size, choice of ingredients etc. Revisit the Fact Cards on Italy and display by the map.

Revisit the learning objective and self assess their learning using Steps to Success.

Next Steps/Home Learning

D&T: Cooking and Nutrition: Use your ingredients to make your starter. Take a photo. Taste, evaluate and consider how it could be improved.
English: Plan and record your starter as a recipe using English skills, e.g. imperative verbs and recount skills, time connectives and appropriate verbs, for the class Italian cookery book.
Home Learning: Make your Italian starter at home and treat your family.

Resources/Facts for the Teacher

Shopping bags containing packets/ pictures of foodstuff that traditionally come from other countries e.g. fish and chips, pizza, curry etc. Set rings and blank card labels. World Map, Fact Cards on Italy to display, Pictures of Italian foods, Selection of Italian food ingredients to taste e.g. pasta, risotto, bruschetta, Selection of different sized paper plates/ bowls.

Pizza is probably the most famous Italian dish. It is usually baked in a wood-fired oven, a thin dough base loaded with fresh vegetables or thinly sliced ham, salami, artichokes or olives. Calzone is a folded up pizza bread filled with tomatoes, ham, cheese.

Pasta is also very popular and there are more than a hundred different shapes. Lasagna is a layered pasta dish with tomato, mozzarella cheese and minced meat filling. Spaghetti bolognaise is spaghetti with tomatoes, ragu sauce and minced meat.

Pesto is a thick green sauce made by blending olives, basil, olive oil, pine kernels and parmiggiano cheese.

Mozzarella Italian cheese balls, originally made from buffalo milk.

Year 3 History Lesson
Afternoon Tea

Theme/Unit
The Victorians

Lesson Overview
Researching the tradition of afternoon tea during Victorian Times

Learning Objective
To learn about the history of afternoon tea, a food tradition that is still popular today.

Success Criteria
Must: I know that afternoon tea is a British tradition.
Should: I understand how the tradition evolved.
Could: I know how and why afternoon tea became fashionable.

Introduction
Show the children a selection of portrait paintings of ladies and gentlemen having afternoon tea on IWB. View images of afternoon tea in Victorian times online (see web links).

Discuss: What can you see? What are the people doing? What do the paintings have in common? What are the people wearing? When do you think they were painted? Why? Explain that these are all paintings of people having 'Afternoon Tea' in Britain long ago.

Ask if anyone has heard of or had afternoon tea. Show some current hotel advertisements for afternoon tea on IWB. Explain how afternoon tea is a British tradition (i.e. the handing down of beliefs or customs from one generation to the next) and today we are going to do some research to learn about it?

Main Teaching
Question the children on what they want to find out. Encourage/prompt such questions as:
— Where was afternoon tea invented?
— When was it invented?
— Who started it?
— Why did they invent it?
— Who was the monarch at the time?
— Who had afternoon tea in the old days?
— Where was it served?
— What was a typical menu?
— Why was it so popular?
— Where did the tea come from?

Record the questions on the IWB. Present the children with a variety of sources to help them find the answers to the questions. Explore how they might use the sources to research and find the answers to the questions.

Teacher Led and Independent Group Tasks
Organise the list of questions into numbered sections and assign each section to a mixed ability group. Their task is to research the answers to those specific questions and to record their answers collectively.

Teacher and teaching assistant are to monitor progress and assist groups in their research where necessary.

Mini plenary
Stop and take the time to listen to each other's answers and discuss research methods.

Continue the research
Ask if gas lighting helped promote the tradition.

Extension
What is High Tea?
Who had High Tea?
Why was it called High Tea?
What was on the menu?

Plenary (AfL Focus)
Ask each group to share their questions and answers. Check if any questions were problematic.

Revisit the learning objective and self assess their learning using Steps to Success.

Watch a film about the Origins of Afternoon Tea (see web links).

Next Steps/Home Learning
D&T: Cooking and Nutrition: Model and make tea, sandwiches, scones and cakes for a whole class afternoon tea.
Home Learning: Share what you have learnt about afternoon tea with your family. Perhaps you can bake a cake and have your own afternoon tea.

Resources/Facts for the Teacher
Use online resources (see web links).

Afternoon tea was invented by Anna, the Seventh Duchess of Bedford in 1840, as a way to offset 'a sinking feeling' she got mid-afternoon between lunch and dinner. At first the Duchess had servants sneak a pot of tea and some sandwiches to her room. On occasion friends would join her. Soon afternoon tea became very popular among the Victorian elite.

Afternoon tea was initially served between 3 and 4 o'clock. It was usually taken at low tea tables in the garden, dining room or parlor. The finest china, silver cutlery and linens were used. The menu consisted of tea, a selection of finger sandwiches, scones with preserves and clotted cream and cakes, to be eaten in that order.

Tea was a very precious commodity in Victorian times. It was imported from India and China and transported in sailing ships called clippers. When Queen Victoria took afternoon tea it was on a very grand scale and became known as a tea reception.

As afternoon tea grew in popularity among the elite in Victorian society High Tea developed among the working class. High Tea is a blend of afternoon tea and supper, it soon replaced the evening meal for many working class families.

It got its name High Tea because it was served between 4 and 5 o'clock in the day, what was considered the high time of the day. In the early days it was taken in tea shops from high stools at counters or standing at a street stall. During the Industrial Revolution, when working conditions were poor, many working families would come home too tired to prepare a meal. Instead they would have High Tea at the dining table set with cold meats, bread, pickles and cheese to eat. Nowadays afternoon tea is usually enjoyed as a celebration for a special event such as a birthday.

Year 4 Lesson Overview

Subject	Learning Objectives	Curriculum Links	Cross Curricular Links	Page Numbers
Maths Roman Gingerbread Area	To find the area of rectilinear shapes.	**Ma4/2.3 Multiplication & Division** Ma4/2.3a recall multiplication and division facts for multiplication tables up to 12 × 12 Ma4/2.3d multiply two-digit and three-digit numbers by a one-digit number using formal written layout **Ma4/3.1 Measurement** Ma4/3.1c find the area of rectilinear shapes by counting squares	D&T: Cooking & Nutrition	82, 83, 84
English Food Revolution	To plan a persuasive letter to the Prime Minister.	**En4/1 Spoken Language** En4/1k consider and evaluate different viewpoints, attending to and building on the contributions of others **En4/3.3 Composition** En4/3.3a Plan their writing by: discussing writing similar to that which they are planning to write in order to understand and learn from its structure, vocabulary and grammar discussing and recording ideas En4/3.3b Draft and write by: composing and rehearsing sentences orally (including dialogue), progressively building a varied and rich vocabulary and an increasing range of sentence structures in non-narrative material, using simple organisational devices En4/3.3c Evaluate and edit by: assessing the effectiveness of their own and others' writing and suggesting improvements **En4/3.4 Vocabulary, grammar & punctuation** En4/3.4a develop their understanding of the concepts by: extending the range of sentences with more than one clause by using a wider range of conjunctions, including when, if, because, although	History, D&T: Cooking and Nutrition	85, 86, 87

Subject	Learning Objectives	Curriculum Links	Cross Curricular Links	Page Numbers
Science Changing Foods	To find out what happens to foods when they are heated and cooled.	**Sc4/1 Working Scientifically** Sc4/1.3 making systematic and careful observations and, where appropriate, taking accurate measurements using standard units, using a range of equipment, including thermometers and data loggers **Sc4/3.1 States of Matter** Sc4/3.1a compare and group materials together, according to whether they are solids, liquids or gases Sc4/3.1b observe that some materials change state when they are heated or cooled, and measure or research the temperature at which this happens in degrees Celsius (°C)	Maths, D&T: Cooking & Nutrition	88, 89, 90
Geography Fairtrade Bananas	To find out where our food comes from.	**Ge2/1.1 Locational Knowledge** Ge2/1.1a locate the world's countries, using maps to focus on Europe (including the location of Russia) and North and South America, concentrating on their environmental regions, key physical and human characteristics, countries, and major cities **Ge2/1.3 Human and Physical Geography** Ge2/1.3b describe and understand key aspects of human geography, including: types of settlement and land use, economic activity including trade links, and the distribution of natural resources including energy, food, minerals and water **Ge2/1.4 Geographical Skills and Fieldwork** Ge2/1.4a use maps, atlases, globes and digital/ computer mapping to locate countries and describe features studied	English, D&T: Cooking & Nutrition, Citizenship & PSHE	91, 92, 93

Year 4 Maths Lesson
Roman Gingerbread Area

Theme/Unit
Romans

Lesson Overview
Children to use the Roman defence technique of the tortoise to explore area.

Previous Learning
Maths: Finding the perimeter.
History: The Roman Army.

Learning Objective
To find the area of rectilinear shapes.

Success Criteria
Must: I understand what area is.
Should: I can find the area of a rectilinear shape by counting squares units.
Could: I can use the L x W formula to find the area of a rectilinear shape.

Introduction
Revisit square numbers. Display a pattern of large counters, e.g. 1, 2x2, 3x3. Ask the children if they can see a pattern. Can they write a number sentence for each pattern? Can they continue the pattern on their whiteboards? Elicit that these are square numbers and can be written 1x1= 1 or 1^2 , 2x2= 4 or 2^2, 3x3= 9 or 3^2. How far can they calculate?

Look at a 100 square on the IWB (see web links). Can they shade in the square numbers? Look at a multiplication square (see web links). Can they shade in the square numbers? Ask what they notice. Ask if the patterns remind them of the tortoise formations the Roman legionaries used to defend themselves.

Main Teaching

Question the children on what they know about the Roman soldiers and the Roman army (See Facts for Teacher). Explain how the tortoise arrangement was successful because using the shields this way covered the greatest surface area and gave the soldiers the most protection.

Using large sheets of card as shields encourage some children to join forces to protect themselves. Consider various configurations of two shields, three shields etc. in an effort to give the greatest protection or cover the greatest area. Discuss.

Study a shield. Introduce the concept of area as the space inside the shield/rectangle and elicit how best to measure it. Have one sheet of card ruled in square units. Ask the children to count the squared units together and thereby find the area of the shield. Enquire what area two shields would cover. What area would three shields cover? How could they find out? Discuss.

Draw the children's attention to the squares inside the rectangle again. Note they cover the surface of the shape, they are all the same size and fit perfectly together covering the surface. They are congruent.

Display some rectilinear shapes. Model finding the area by counting the squares within together (possibly putting the numbers in as they go to avoid recounting) and agree the area of each shape in square units.

Re-establish area as the space inside the shape that is measured in square units before showing some examples of arrays e.g. an egg box, a baking tray or a Lego brick. Elicit the number sentences to match the arrays. Display a rectangle, measuring 5 squares by 9 squares. Ask the children to record the appropriate number sentence for the array e.g. 5x9=45.

Enquire if this strategy can be used to measure the area of a rectilinear shape. Model counting the squares within the rectangle as before. Confirm the area = 45 square units. Deduce that area = Length x Width (LXW) and is measured in squared units.

Give each child a sheet of cm squared paper to examine and explain that the units we use for measuring area are square centimetres or cm^2 if the area is small e.g. a book or a place mat. Record square centimetres = cm^2

Explore some examples of rectilinear shapes drawn on the cm^2 paper and establish how best to record the area e.g. Area = 28 cm^2

Ensure the children are clear about how to find the area of a shape and what unit of measure to use.

Teacher Led and Independent Group Tasks Task

Draw a template for a Roman shield ginger biscuit on cm^2 paper, find its area and use it to complete challenge cards.

(BA) Teaching Assistant to work with this group, each to draw and cut out a Roman shield (rectangle) measuring 10cm x 8cm. Encourage the children to find the area of each shield by counting squares and record in cm^2. Working pairs find the area of two shields and similarly of three? Change the configuration. Is the area still the same? Can they create a tortoise formation and find its area?

(A) These groups to work initially in pairs or small groups to draw and cut out Roman shields measuring 12cm x 9cm. Children then to work independently counting squares to complete the challenge cards (see Facts for Teacher).

(HA) Teacher to work with this group. Can they draw as many shields as possible with an area of 96 cm^2.

Encourage them to choose a shield to investigate e.g. to combine with another at their table to find the area of the composite shape. Suggest they try to use the formula (LxW) to complete the challenge, record their answers and create some challenges of their own.

Plenary (AfL Focus)
Share the learning. Consider how uniform the shields are. Read a selection of challenges and compare answers. Piece together congruent shields to form different configurations. Find their combined area. Listen to the children's own challenges. Discuss.

Encourage the children to sit with a partner, combine shields with different areas to form composite shapes and find their areas. Revisit the learning objective and self assess their learning using Steps to Success.

Next Steps/Home Learning
D&T: Cooking & Nutrition: Make and bake Roman shield biscuits out of gingerbread using the template. Compare the area of the template and the cooked biscuit. Has baking the biscuit altered the area?
Maths: Design rectilinear Roman mosaics using 1cm squared gummed shapes or sticks and measure the area.

Resources/Facts for the Teacher
IWB, WBs and pens, counters, square paper flip chart, baking tray, egg box, Lego brick, several large sheets of card for Roman shields, sheets of cm2 paper, differentiated challenge cards e.g.

Challenge I
You are a soldier in the Roman Army.
Find the area of your shield to learn how much protection your shield will give you in battle.
Area = _____ cm²

Challenge Ii
You and 3 other soldiers are cut off from the rest of your legion during battle and you are now at risk. Find the combined area of your shields to gauge how much protection you have.
Area = _____ cm²

Challenge III
You are a member of the contubernium (8 soldiers). You have been sent on ahead by the centurion but have strayed into enemy territory. Find the combined area of your shields to gauge how much protection your tortoise defence will give you.
Area = _____ cm²

A square number is a number multiplied by itself.

Area is the amount of space inside the perimeter of a shape. (Area = L X W)

Area is measured in square centimetres, square metres or square kilometres.

In geometry, if two shapes are the same shape and size they are congruent.

Arrays are pictorial representations that help us understand multiplication.

Rectilinear shapes are shapes made up of straight lines and angular corners.

Roman soldiers used a short sword, daggers and a long spear as weapons. They wore metal armour and protected themselves with a large shield. When in battle they would put their shields up all around them to protect themselves from their enemies' arrows. This formation was called a tortoise.

Year 4 English Lesson
Food Revolution

Theme/Unit
Revolution

Lesson Overview
To plan a persuasive letter to the Prime Minister.

Previous Learning
English: The characteristics of persuasive texts using food adverts.
History: The French Revolution.

Learning Objectives
Children to join in the food revolution by planning a persuasive letter to the Prime Minister asking him/her to actively promote healthy breakfasts.

Success Criteria
Must: I can write a persuasive letter.
Should: I can develop and support my arguments.
Could: I can use emotive language and techniques.

Introduction
Display examples of 'good' and 'bad' breakfasts (poster/IWB) and discuss (see web links).

Consider the importance of breakfast, the health benefits and the need to be better informed (see web links).

Explain how the breakfast picture is part of a bigger campaign being run by Jamie Oliver called the Food Revolution. Ask the children what they already know about Jamie Oliver. Elicit his mission to help people to eat more healthily. List/ elicit some of the things he does and has done e.g. recipe books (see Facts for Teacher).

Main Teaching

Incite the children to actively join the food revolution. Elicit how e.g. make better food choices, design and display posters, grow food, suggest food choices at home, to friends etc.

Refer to Jamie Oliver's lobbying of the government to introduce a sugar tax (see web links).

Suggest they plan a persuasive letter to the Prime Minister promoting healthy breakfasts. Discuss the structure of a letter and model a template on the IWB. Tease out ideas with the children and annotate the template e.g. firstly, in addition and furthermore as paragraph starters. Agree on an address and who to write to e.g. The Prime Minister, 10 Downing Street, London.

Be clear on the point of the letter e.g. I am writing to ensure all breakfasts are healthy. Explore their suggestions for their three arguments. Can they develop them? Can they support them with evidence? Can they reiterate their point, summarise their arguments and suggest a possible solution or a way forward? Do they know how to end a letter?

Next consider the children's choice of language for a 'persuasive' letter and record on the IWB. Build some 'convincing' word banks e.g.

Using the breakfast poster as a stimulus encourage some volunteers to voice possible paragraphs of a letter. They can refer to the word banks to if required.

Teacher Led and Independent Group Tasks

Task: Plan a persuasive letter to the Prime Minister promoting healthy breakfasts.

(BA) Teaching Assistant to work with this group to each plan a letter to the Prime Minister. Show the poster again. Discuss 'good' breakfasts versus 'bad' breakfasts. Listen to the children's points of view. Can they develop them? Ask what the Prime Minister can do to help. Give each child a letter template to use as a framework. Question them on what needs to be completed in each section e.g. they need to clearly write the point of their letter in the introduction. Talk through their ideas as they write. Encourage them to use the word banks and include persuasive language. Assist where necessary.

(A) Children to work quite independently. Give them a poster to share and discuss initially with a partner and a letter template to use to shape their letter. Remind them of the purpose of the letter and encourage them to use the word banks to include persuasive language.

(HA) Teacher to work with this group. Consider the poster, the point of the letter, their arguments and how they can support them.

Connectives	Strong Adjectives	Powerful Verbs	Emotive language	Persuasive Starters
Firstly	fresh	support	Obviously you ...	The fact is ...
In addition	real (truth)	highlight	Clearly this is ...	Surely you know ...
Furthermore	well-balanced	refuel	It is irresponsible ...	All the evidence suggests ...
however, although, if	nutritious	crave	Only this could	Most people would agree ...

Encourage them to structure their letter based on the template and use emotive, persuasive language. Suggest using a rhetorical question in one of their arguments to gain more effect.

Plenary (AfL Focus)
Share the learning: Display the breakfast poster and listen to each other's letters. Discuss and evaluate. Does the persuasive letter have...?

structure of a letter		connectives	
clear point		persuasive starters	
three developed arguments		strong adjectives and powerful verbs	
summary and possible course of action		emotive language	

Highlight the use of a rhetorical question.

Revisit the learning objective and self assess their learning using Steps to Success.

Next Steps/Home Learning
English: Edit, redraft and best copy the persuasive letters.
D&T: Cooking and Nutrition: Design and make two breakfasts: one an energy boosting breakfast and the other a typical breakfast that doesn't boost energy. Take photographs.
D&T: Use the photographs to design 'Feed the Future Breakfast Awareness' posters for school, home and the locality.

ICT: Email letters to friends, family and partnership schools and invite them to join the Food Revolution.
Home Learning: Suggest some alternative healthy breakfast options at home.

Resources/Facts for the Teacher
IWB, some breakfast foods, Jamie Oliver recipe books, copies of a letter template, paper copies of the 'Breakfast: Eat A Breakfast' poster.

On Friday 20th May 2016 Jamie Oliver, chef, restaurateur and healthy food champion, launched his Food Revolution.

His aim is to make real, long-lasting changes to what we eat and he wants everyone on board to help.
He has a multi-pronged approach to making a difference: he delights in cooking and sharing healthy and delicious recipes; he draws public attention to the 'ugly truths' of the food industry and he engages with government to make changes. He has published several cookery books and produced corresponding TV cookery programmes. Many years ago he attempted to improve school dinners. More recently he lobbied government to introduce a sugar tax. He has adopted the sugar tax in his own restaurants and other restaurants have followed suit. The money gained is donated to Sustain, an organisation that promotes good farming practices that produce quality foodstuffs.

Year 4 Science Lesson
Changing Foods

Theme/Unit
States of Matter

Lesson Overview
Children to carry out investigations to see how foodstuffs change state when they are heated and cooled.

Previous Learning
Science: Compare and group materials into solids, liquids and gases.

Learning Objective
To find out what happens to foods when they are heated and cooled.

Success Criteria
Must: I know the three states of matter.
Should: I know that foods can change state when heated and cooled.
Could: I can measure the temperature at which a change occurs in °C.

Introduction
Elicit the names of the three states of matter. Present Characteristics of Matter Cards (see web links). Shuffle them and deal them out, one to each child. Can they, in turn, read their cards and match the characteristic to the state of matter label?

Main Teaching

Consider solids and their characteristics. Ask the children if they know a solid that can change its state. Listen to their suggestions and explanations. Similarly explore liquids and gases and their characteristics.

Choose water as a material. Demonstrate heating water using a kettle whilst questioning the children. What state of matter is water? What happens if water is heated? What state will it change into? At what temperature does water boil? Model using a thermometer to confirm the °C. Establish that water (a liquid) when heated changes into vapour (evaporation) and record on the IWB.

Remind children about health and safety in the kitchen when heating materials.
Enquire if the process can be reversed i.e. Can vapour become liquid? Using a saucepan lid demonstrate how water vapour, when cooled, can change state into a liquid. Establish that vapour when cooled changes into liquid (condensation) and record this process on the IWB.

Ask what happens when water is cooled. Elicit water changes into ice when frozen. Place some water in an ice cube tray and put in the freezer. Elicit the fact that water freezes at 0°C. Establish that a liquid when cooled changes into a solid (freezing) and record on the IWB. Enquire if this process can be reversed i.e. Can a solid become a liquid?
Establish that a solid when heated changes into a liquid (melting) and record on the IWB.

Reconsider the four processes on the IWB and group them into two groups: heating and cooling.
Through quick-fire questioning ensure the children understand that water and other materials change state when heated and cooled.

Teacher Led and Independent Group Tasks

In the kitchen present the children with a selection of foods and a question to investigate:
What happens when we heat and cool these foodstuffs?

Have a number of 'Heating and Cooling Stations' pre-set up in the kitchen e.g. bread to toast, chocolate to melt, pasta to boil, eggs to poach, water to boil, make a squash lolly in a mould to freeze, ice cream to melt, jelly to make, grapes to freeze, peas to freeze.

Organise the children into small mixed ability groups so each group can investigate one heating and one cooling investigation. They must record their findings clearly using scientific language, drawings and/or labelled diagrams, e.g. solid chocolate when heated melts and becomes runny (liquid). When cooled the process is reversed i.e. runny liquid becomes solid again. Display findings.

Talk through what materials and equipment are at each station. Elicit what the children might do to answer the question. Clarify teacher expectations.

(BA) To find out how foodstuff changes when it is heated and cooled.

(A) As above, but consider whether or not the change can be reversed.

(HA) Find out how food changes when it is heated and cooled, whether or not the change can be reversed and at what temperature the change takes place.

Remind the children about health and safety in the kitchen before beginning the investigation. Teacher, Teaching Assistant and parent helpers to supervise the heating stations.

Plenary (AfL Focus)

Give the children some time to walk around and consider the other investigations and their recorded findings. Remember the foods in the freezer.

Afterwards encourage each group to report their findings to the class. Discuss and compare results. Look at the whether or not the changes were reversible e.g. bread to toast. Were there any surprises? Note at what temperatures the changes took place. Draw class conclusions and peer assess: e.g. most solids melt into liquids when heated, a gas condenses into a liquid when cooled, liquids evaporate into gas when heated and a liquid freezes into a solid when it is cooled.

Conclude the lesson looking at the range of temperatures at which various materials change state (see web links).

Next Steps/Home Learning

Science: e: Use the recorded findings to create an information table using scientific language entitled 'What happens when we heat and cool these foodstuffs?' Draw a line graph to show the various temperatures at which the foods change state.

Home Learning: ing: At meal times consider how your food changes before and after preparation.

Resources/Facts for the Teacher

IWB, name cards for states of matter (solid, liquid, gas), characteristics of states of matter cards, access to water supply, kettle, hot plates, thermometers, ice cubes, access to a freezer, materials to investigate (potatoes, bread, chocolate, pasta, squash, eggs, ice cream, jelly, grapes, peas), kitchen utensils (clear, heat resistant bowls, saucepans, spoons to stir, cutting tools and chopping boards, toaster, silicone poaching pod, ice lolly moulds, small freezer bags).

There are three states of matter: solid, liquid, and gas. Temperature is the measure of how hot or cold something is. The unit of measure is degrees Celsius (°C). When water, a liquid, is heated until it boils it changes into water vapour, a gas. This process is called evaporation. When the water vapour, a gas, is cooled it changes into water, a liquid. This process is called condensation. When water, a liquid, is cooled it changes into ice, a solid. The process is called freezing. When ice, a solid, is heated it changes into water, a liquid. This process is called melting. Water boils at 100 °C. Water freezes at 0°C.

Year 4 Geography Lesson
Fairtrade Bananas

Theme/Unit
South America

Lesson Overview
Children to learn about the pros of fair trade as experienced by a fair trade banana farmer and his family in Columbia.

Learning Objective
To find out where our food comes from.

Success Criteria
Must: I know where bananas come from.
Should: I understand about fair trade.
Could: I know how I can make a difference.

Introduction
Give the children a selection of foodstuffs, some of which have the Fairtrade Mark, to sort as they see fit. Teacher then to sort into 'fair trade' and 'not fair trade' sets and elicit why.

Ask if they have seen the Fairtrade Mark before and know what it means (see Facts for Teacher). Establish what they understand by fair, trade and fair trade.

Focusing on the fair trade foodstuffs find out where they have come from and have children locate the countries on globes and in atlases before finding on a world map on the IWB. Can they spot a trend? For example, where are most of the 'growing' countries in the world and why?

Main Teaching

Focus on Columbia in South America, where growing bananas is a big business.

Watch a film about making bananas fair (see web links) to find out: How many bananas a day are eaten in Britain? How being a fair trade farmer helps farmers to support their families? Who is making life difficult for the farmer?Listen to what the children have learnt. Discuss.

In pairs ask the children to draft a list of incentives on their WBs that a Fairtrade farmer could use to persuade his neighbouring farmers to become fair trade farmers. Give some direction e.g. regular pay, working conditions, access to education etc. (see Facts for Teacher). Reconvene, pool ideas and discuss. Record on the IWB.

Refer to a World map and find all the banana growing countries of the world (see web links). Enquire how they think they could make a difference and help fair trade farmers around the world.Suggest they host a Fair Trade Awareness Day in school and listen to the children's suggestions.

Teacher Led and Independent Group Tasks

Task: Plan a Fair Trade Awareness Day for school.

(BA) This group is to work with a Teaching Assistant to design and make a card game to sort: Fair Trade Versus Not Fair Trade. Elicit the children's understanding of fair trade and talk about how being a fair trade farmer has improved many farmers lives. Using the list on the IWB their challenge is to:
Make some cards highlighting the advantages of being a fair trade farmer e.g. Farmers get a fair price for the crops they grow (certainty).

Make some cards highlighting the plight of the farmer who is not a fair trade farmer e.g. Farmers don't know whether they will even be paid (uncertainty).

Discuss ideas for board design and create it.

(A) Teacher to work with these groups to design and make Fair Trade Awareness posters to distribute around the school. Challenge them to consider the Fairtrade Mark in their design and the pros and cons of being a fair trade farmer. Ensure they consider their audience and include a clear message/catchy slogan; bold writing; persuasive text with pictures that tell a story, facts and possibly a celebrity quote or endorsement.

(HA) This group is to work independently to design and create a power point presentation on fair trade that they can deliver at a whole school assembly on Fair Trade Awareness Day. Their challenge is to present and explain the concept of fair trade simply using facts and pictures; show how lives are better for those who are fair trade farmers and highlight how we can help the fair trade movement.

Plenary (AfL Focus)

Share the learning: Play the board game, evaluate the posters and watch the presentation. Revisit the learning objective and self assess their learning using Steps to Success. Plan the next steps to making Fair Trade Awareness Day effective.

Next Steps/Home Learning

Geography: Trace the journey of the banana. Consider all the people involved and their roles. Make sandwich boards for each of them. Create a human food chain e.g. from the banana farmer (who grows the bananas), to the plantation owner, the van driver, packer, to shipper, to distributor, to us (who eat bananas as healthy snacks). Consider how we are all inextricably linked (see web links).

D&T: Cooking and Nutrition: Use some fair trade products to make some snacks to distribute on Fair Trade Awareness Day.

Home Learning: Talk about fair trade at home and suggest adding some fair trade items to the weekly shopping list.

Resources/Facts for the Teacher

IWB, WBs and pens, food stuff to sort (some of which have fair trade stickers), sorting rings, globes, atlases, card for games, poster paper, access to laptops and the internet.

Fair: It is fair that everything is equal or it is fair if everyone gets what they need.

Trade is about buying and selling products. Fair trade is all about giving the people who produce the things you buy a fair price for their work.

Fairtrade Mark is a registered trade mark. The symbol depicts a blue sky to symbolise optimism, a raised arm to symbolise empowerment and the colour green is used to symbolise growth. One in three bananas bought in the Britain has the Fairtrade Mark. The price of a banana bought in a British supermarket has dropped in price over the last ten years. This means that farmers and workers in countries like Columbia cannot sustain a livelihood growing bananas.

If we buy Fairtrade bananas in the Britain then farmers are guaranteed: regular income; guaranteed work, trading contracts so they can plan for their future; organisations that can support them; fair trade premium to invest in their community; good housing; education for their children; health care; better working conditions; health and safety standards, their rights are respected; men and women are treated equally; there is no child labour; harmful chemicals are not used to increase production; the environment is cared for and people have control over their own lives.

Year 5 Lessons

Maths
English
Science
Art & Design

Year 5 Lesson Overview

Subject	Learning Objectives	Curriculum Links	Cross Curricular Links	Page Numbers
Maths Anglo-Saxon Fractions	To collect and record data. To find fractions of amounts.	**Ma5/2.3 Multiplication & Division** Ma5/2.3e multiply and divide numbers mentally drawing upon known facts. Ma5/2.3k solve problems involving multiplication and division, including scaling by simple fractions and problems involving simple rates. **Ma5/2.4 Fractions** (decimals & percentages) Ma5/2.4f read and write decimal numbers as fractions. **Ma5/4.1 Statistics** Ma5/4.1b complete, read and interpret information in tables, including timetables.	English, History, D&T: Cooking and Nutrition	98, 99, 100
English Dinner in Space	To research and plan a delicious and nutritious meal for a dinner party in space.	**En5/1 Spoken Language** En5/1c use relevant strategies to build their vocabulary En5/1d articulate and justify answers, arguments and opinions **En5/2.2 Comprehension** En5/2.2e retrieve, record and present information from non-fiction **En5/3.3 Composition** En5/3.3a Plan their writing by: i. identifying the audience for and purpose of the writing, selecting the appropriate form and using other similar writing as models for their own ii. noting and developing initial ideas, drawing on reading and research where necessary.	Science, Maths, D&T: Cooking and Nutrition	101, 102, 103

Subject	Learning Objectives	Curriculum Links		Cross Curricular Links	Page Numbers
Science Separating Mixtures	To understand different methods for separating mixtures.	**Sc5/3.1 Properties and Changes of Materials** Sc5/3.1b know that some materials will dissolve in liquid to form a solution, and describe how to recover a substance from a solution. Sc5/3.1c use knowledge of solids, liquids and gases to decide how mixtures might be separated, including through filtering, sieving and evaporating. Sc5/3.1e demonstrate that dissolving, mixing and changes of state are reversible changes.		Maths, D&T: Cooking and Nutrition	104, 105, 106
Art & Design Natural Dyes	To dye yarn using naturally made dyes.	Pupils should be taught to develop their **techniques**, including their control and their use of materials, with creativity, experimentation and an increasing awareness of different kinds of art, craft and design.		History, Science, Maths, D&T: Cooking and Nutrition	107, 108, 109

Year 5 Maths Lesson
Anglo-Saxon Fractions

Theme/Unit
Anglo-Saxons

Lesson Overview
To use mathematical skills to calculate the amounts of ingredients needed to prepare recipes for an Anglo-Saxon class feast.

Previous Learning
History: Research and collect a variety of recipes for an Anglo-Saxon feast.

Learning Objectives
To find fractions of amounts.
To collect and record data.

Success Criteria
Must: I can collect data and find fractions of amounts.
Should: I can apply these skills confidently.
Could: I can explain how I achieved my calculations.

Introduction
Play a Bingo game to practise finding fractions of amounts and measures, e.g. grams and millilitres (see web links). Use WBs to record answers.

Recap briefly on previous learning, questioning the children on what they know about Anglo-Saxon food (see Facts for Teacher).

Consider the variety of recipes they have researched and the seasonal fruit and vegetables available.

Explain they are going to begin to prepare for a feast. Agree on a set menu for the feast e.g. a choice of two starters, a choice of two mains and bread, a choice of two desserts and perhaps a drink.

Main Teaching

Begin by considering the number of guests at the feast (class of 30) and consequently the need to know the amount of each dish required.

Elicit the need to collect data and an appropriate method e.g. tally chart. Encourage groups to choose a dish to prepare/assign dishes to groups. Revise through questioning what each group needs to do before collecting their data.

Mini Activity: Each group to collect data so they know how many people to prepare their dish for and record on a WB. Reconvene and consider the data collected e.g. make sure everyone has ordered a starter, a main course some bread, a dessert and a drink, and the numbers tally. Using the children's suggestions design a single tally chart to incorporate all the choices.

Now suggest a recipe e.g. kale soup as a starter. Display the recipe on the IWB (see Facts for Teacher). Read through the ingredients.

Consider the units of measurement used for each of the ingredients and through questioning briefly recap on previous learning e.g. grams (g) are a measure of mass in the metric system, 1000g = 1 kilogram (kg), millilitres (ml) are a measure of capacity/volume, 1000 mi = 1 litre (l), 500ml = 0.5 l etc.

Refer back to the class tally chart and consider the number of orders for the starter e.g. kale soup for 12 children.

Ask the children to consider the recipe and the number of orders. What do they notice? Elicit the need to use mathematical skills to adapt the amount of each ingredient needed within the recipe so there is enough. Suggest they prepare the soup for 12 people and

encourage them to record the amount of each ingredient needed independently on their WBs. Consider how the recipe says (5 to 6) helpings. Discuss. Listen to their answers. Ask if they can they explain how they calculated them e.g. multiply each ingredient by 2 or double each ingredient. Continue as above suggesting 18/24/30 children wanted kale soup. (Assign a quantity to particular groups). Then suggest only 3 children wanted the kale soup and ask how they might calculate the correct amount of each ingredient.

Listen to the children's answers. Encourage them to show on their WBs how they calculated them and explain what operation and strategy they used e.g. find ½ of each ingredient or divide by 2. Similarly suggest only 2 children wanted kale soup i.e. find ⅓ of each ingredient. Ask how to find out how much of each ingredient would be needed if 4 children wanted kale soup. Continue as above practising finding fractions of amounts.

Teacher Led and Independent Group Tasks

Reiterate the need to change each recipe to meet the food requirements on the class tally. Set the task: Can you work out the correct amount of ingredients needed for your recipe?

(BA) TA to work with this group on both starter recipes. Encourage the group to work together initially to change the amounts of ingredients needed for the first starter on their WBs and explain what how they calculated the changes. Then set them the task of working more independently to change the amount of ingredients needed for the second recipe. Assist where necessary. Record.

(A) Each of three groups to work as a group on changing the amounts of ingredients for each of the desserts and the bread/ breads. Record. Teacher to move between the groups and assist where necessary.

(HA) This group to work in pairs to change the amounts of ingredients needed for each of the main courses and the drink. Record.

Plenary (AfL Focus)

Children to share their learning with the group checking each recipe is sufficient to meet the orders. Discuss methods used.

Revisit the learning objective and self assess their learning using Steps to Success.

Suggest that the next step before preparing the feast is to create a class shopping list based on all their requirements. Elicit how best to collect this information and record it e.g. a tally.

Next Steps/Home Learning

D&T: Cooking and Nutrition: Prepare and cook an Anglo-Saxon Feast.
Home Learning: Help prepare a family meal at home. Adapt and measure the ingredients accordingly.

Resources/Facts for the Teacher

A selection of previously researched Anglo-Saxon recipes (see web links), IWB, individual WBs and pens, metric tables for reference.

The Anglo-Saxons liked to eat and drink and often gathered for feasts in the Hall. They cooked their food over open fires set in the middle of the house.
While they sometimes roasted meat (deer, wild boar, pig meat) over the fires they were largely vegetarian.

They grew and ate cereals (wheat and rye for bread, barley for brewing and oats for porridge), vegetables (peas, beans, onions, cabbages, carrots and parsnips) and fruits (apples, pears, plums, strawberries, blackberries, and cherries). Animals were mainly kept for their produce e.g. chickens for eggs, sheep for wool etc.

They caught and ate fish cooked over the open fires. They drank a weak beer made from barley and mead (a honey sweetened beer) because water was impure and wine had to be imported so was expensive.

A fraction is part of a whole/quantity. When converting decimals to fractions find the denominator and then cancel down if possible e.g. $0.1 = \frac{1}{10}$, $0.5 = \frac{5}{10} = \frac{1}{2}$

Kale Soup Recipe

Ingredients: (serves 5 to 6)
250g kale
50g leek
knob of butter
½ an onion
0.5 litres of vegetable stock
125g of fried bacon bits
125 ml of cream

Year 5 English Lesson
Dinner In Space

Theme/Unit
The Space Race

Lesson Overview
Consider the nutritional value of foods while planning a meal for a party in space.

Previous Learning
History: The history of space travel.

Learning Objective
To research and plan a delicious and nutritious meal for a dinner party in space.

Success Criteria
Must: I can plan and write a recipe.
Should: I can use other sources to research the topic.
Could: I can use the information gathered to inform and develop my own ideas.

Introduction
Play the class game ' I am going on a mission into space so I need to pack...' Once everyone has had a turn group suggestions into categories e.g. equipment, clothes, food etc. Focus on food choices and ask what food the children would miss most.

Explain how the European Space Agency (ESA) has estimated that each astronaut on the International Space Station (ISS) needs 5kg of food and water every day. Use a scales and food to show 5kg.

Briefly discuss the importance and problems of supplying good quality food for astronauts in space.

Main Teaching

Show some samples of space food. Explain how it is freeze-dried. Elicit the children's understanding (see Facts for Teacher). Encourage the children to examine and describe the dehydrated foodstuff and then sample, by rehydrating, and describe how it tastes and feels compared to its initial texture. Were they surprised?

Explain how textures add interest to our food e.g. imagine if all of our meals were drinks or just mush. Elicit and list adjectives that describe texture e.g. juicy apple, crunchy nuts, crumbly cheese etc.

Show a variety of foodstuffs to sample e.g. grapes, crackers, yogurt, raisins, chocolate buttons and bread. Encourage the children to describe the textures.

Compare the texture between different forms of the same food e.g. firm strawberry versus runny strawberry jam or wobbly jelly, or a crisp apple versus gooey apple sauce.

Display a picture of Captain Tim Peake and discuss his mission to the International Space Station (see web links). Query what food he might have eaten and missed.

Show the children the press release of The Great British Space Dinner Competition that was launched in May 2014, before Tim Peake went on his mission (see web links). Encourage them to read about the competition in pairs and retrieve and highlight/note significant details. (What was the competition aiming to achieve? What were the requirements? What are the nutritional principles? What constraints might space travel cause?) Discuss.

Elicit the children's understanding of nutrition and the four main food groups – Protein, Fats, Carbohydrates, Vitamins and Mineral (what our bodies need for a well-balanced diet). Discuss their benefits.

Speak to the children about sugar and how it is important not to eat more than 6 teaspoons in a day. Honey might be a good Space Food as it never goes off. It has an eternal shelf life if its in an airtight container.

Invite children to share their favourite meals and check if they are nutritionally well-balanced and have a variety of textures.

Teacher Led and Independent Group Tasks

Research and plan a delicious and nutritious meal for a dinner party in space. Supplying tasty nutritional food for astronauts is a constant dilemma. While in Space there are other constraints. Elicit the children's ideas e.g. low gravity, helmets etc. (see web links).

(BA) TA to work with this group to come up with an idea for a meal. Look at some recipe cards and books for ideas. Consider the style of recipe writing. Listen to each other's suggestions. Consider the flavours. Aim to vary the textures. Agree on a meal. Record the ingredients. Write the recipe. Discuss the nutritional value of the meal and annotate the recipe.

(A) Teacher to work with these small groups, as above.

(HA) This group to work in a small group, quite independently, researching their ideas, making choices and planning their space meals as above.

Extension
Think about how your meal would be packaged for space travel.

Plenary (AfL Focus)
Share ideas. Compare and evaluate the variety of ideas, textures and the nutritional benefits. Revisit the learning objective and self assess their learning using Steps to Success.

Listen to the results of 'The Great British Space Dinner' competition (see web links). Compare meal ideas.

Next Steps/Home Learning
D&T: Cooking and Nutrition: Prepare a space dinner, using own recipe. Season and adapt it showing an awareness of taste, smell and texture.
Science: Consider the possibilities of growing food in Space (see web links).
Home Learning: Think about your daily food choices and how a variety of textures can make your food more interesting.

Resources/Facts for the Teacher
IWB, weighing scales, 5kg of foodstuff, three packets of freeze dried space food (enough for a class to sample) or freeze dried strawberries, food texture samples (e.g. grapes, crackers, yogurt and spoons, raisins, chocolate buttons, bread), highlighter pens, white boards and pens, internet access for research (see web links), a selection of recipe books and recipe cards.

ISS-The International Space Station, ESA- European Space Agency, Space food needs to be good quality, nutritionally balanced food, which is tasty to eat, easy to transport, and can be easily stored while travelling through space.

Nutrition is the study of what our bodies need to grow and stay healthy. It is important to understand how much food we should eat so we do not become overweight or obese as this can lead to increased risk of disease. It's also important not to eat too much sugar in our diets. Sugary drinks are particularly high in sugar. One can have up to 9 teaspoons of sugar in it, which is more than the recommended 6 teaspoons per day for children.

Freeze drying is the process that has been used to store astronaut food safely since early space travel. It entails the food being frozen in a vacuum chamber until the water content crystallises. The air pressure is then lowered forcing the air out of the chamber. Heat is applied which causes the ice to evaporate. Then a freezing coil traps the vaporised water. Eventually the foodstuff is dehydrated or freeze-dried.

Captain Tim Peake was on a mission called Principia to the ISS. He spent 6 months in space (December 2015 to June 2016). While he was there primarily to carry out experiments and new research in science and technology he also had to eat a healthy varied diet, drink and exercise for about two hours a day. Staying healthy in Space is very important as the environment is extreme, the space is limited, microgravity causes loss of bone and muscle density and medical help is very far away.

Year 5 Science Lesson
Separating Mixtures

Theme/Unit
Properties of Materials

Lesson Overview
To know, use and understand a variety of methods used to separate materials when mixed.

Previous Learning
Materials and their properties. Solubility: finding out which materials are soluble and insoluble in water.

Learning Objective
To understand different methods for separating mixtures.

Success Criteria
<u>Must:</u> I know different methods for separating mixtures.
<u>Should:</u> I can choose the appropriate method for the task.
<u>Could:</u> I can explain how the different processes work.

Introduction
Consider the results of the previous lesson's experiments on solubility, where the children tested which materials were soluble and insoluble in water e.g. sand and water, salt and water etc.

Revisit their understanding of soluble and insoluble. Briefly discuss their findings.

Ask the question: Is it possible to separate the materials?

Main Teaching

Begin to introduce the different methods of separating materials in a mixture.

Teacher to add sand to water and discuss.
Ask: Can I reverse the change? How might I separate them? Show filter paper. Elicit filtration. Model and explain the process. Record the definition for filtration and when else it might be used on the IWB (see Facts for Teachers).

Add salt to water. Allow it to dissolve. Discuss.
Ask: Can I reverse the change? How might I separate them? Model and explain the process. Warn about dangers. Elicit evaporation. Record the definition on the IWB.

Ask if the children can think of any everyday situations where solid materials are separated from each other or from liquids? (stones from soil, pasta from water, making tea with a tea bag etc.)

Show the children a selection of everyday items and elicit their function and what they have in common e.g. a selection of sieves (garden, kitchen), a variety of teabags, tea strainers, different sized colanders, nets... Establish that they can all be used to separate materials in mixtures. Elicit key word: sieve. Model an example of sieving with children supporting e.g. sand and gravel. Which sieve would they use? Encourage the children to and explain the process of sieving. Record the definition on the IWB.

Introduce a magnet and ask if and how this could be used to separate materials in a mixture. Discuss its use at a recycling plant. Elicit magnetism as the process of separation. Record the definition on the IWB.

Show a decanter. Explain what it is, how it is usually associated with wine and it gives its name to the process of decanting which is just allowing a mixture of solid and liquid or two immiscible liquids to settle and separate by gravity. Model decanting e.g. oil and water, cream and milk or dirt and water. Record the definition on the IWB.

Teacher Led and Independent Group Tasks

Recap on the different methods of separation and when they might be used. Introduce and explain the activity as three tasks.
Task 1: Make some mixtures.
Task 2: Separate the mixtures.
Task 3: Identify the methods of separation.

Provide a selection of materials and instructions at five 'separating' stations. Place the measuring and separating equipment centrally.

Before beginning highlight the importance of recording test results. Advise the children to prepare a table on which to record their finding (TA to assist where necessary). The children to work in five groups (mixed ability).

Task 1: Each group to make a different mixture, following given instructions e.g. Group 1: Mix 30ml of oil with 100ml of water. Group 2: Mix 100g of pasta with 300g of flour. Group 3: Mix 1 tsp. of salt with 100ml of water. Group 4: Mix 50g of iron filings with 200g of cornflakes. Group 5: Mix 1tbsp of coffee with 300ml of water. On completion groups to swop places for task 2.

Task 2: Each group to separate the mixtures. Consider the mixture and the various methods. Identify the most effective method to use to separate the materials. Choose the appropriate equipment and separate.

Task 3: Each group to move around the classroom and look at the examples of separation. Can they identify which method of separation was used? Refer to definitions on the IWB. Record findings.

(Adult to supervise the use of the hot plate during evaporation).

Plenary (AfL Focus)
What is a mixture? Elicit the different methods that can be used to separate mixtures. Consider the children's finding. Did they manage to reverse the changes? Discuss.

Revisit the learning objective and self assess their learning using Steps to Success.
Introduce the water filter challenge: Show the children some clean water. Make it dirty water (add mud, grit and gravel). Explain that their Home Learning challenge is to design a water filter that will reverse the change, making the dirty water clean again. Model how to use an empty plastic bottle. Elicit some materials they could use e.g. tissue paper, cotton wool, fabric, sand. Warn them against drinking the water, even if they think they have cleaned it!

Next Steps/Home Learning
Science: Reversible and irreversible changes.
Home Learning: Make a water filter.

Resources/Facts for the Teacher
Clear plastic cups, bowls, heat resistant beakers, materials (water, sand, salt, cooking oil, flour pasta, sand, gravel, mud, cornflakes, iron filings, coffee), measuring equipment (ml jugs and weighing scales, tea spoons and table spoons), hot plate (supervised), separating equipment (filter papers, variety of sieves, colanders, magnets, decanter), tea bags, tea strainer, nets, empty plastic bottle, tissue, cotton wool, fabric pieces.

Mixture: When you combine two or more materials, you make a mixture.

Soluble: A solute has dissolved when the solution becomes clear.

Insoluble: A solute hasn't dissolved, the solution remains cloudy and there may be sediment.

Solution: In a solution, the liquid is the solvent and the material dissolving in the liquid is the solute.

Filtration: Can separate solids that are insoluble from a liquid e.g. pasta and water, coffee and water.

Evaporation: Can separate a dissolvable solid from a solution e.g. salt and water, sugar and water.

Magnetism: Can separate magnetic materials from nonmagnetic materials e.g. iron filings from cornflakes.

Decanter: A vessel that is used to the decant a liquid e.g. wine, which may contain sediment.

Decant: A process used to separate two 'immiscible' liquids or a liquid from a solid by carefully pouring off one layer e.g. oil and water, cream and milk, dirt and water.

Immiscible: Oil and water don't mix so they are immiscible.

For additional reference material see web links.

Year 5 Art & Design Lesson
Natural Dyes

Theme/Unit
Anglo-Saxons

Lesson Overview
Children dye yarn while exploring the age old process of making dyes from natural produce.

Previous Learning
Revisit where wool comes from and how yarn is spun. In pairs, make skeins of yarn, wash them and hang to dry (use 100 grams of wool per skein).

Learning Objective
To dye yarn using naturally made dyes.

Success Criteria
Must: I can make a dyebath and dye yarn.
Should: I know how to vary the intensity of colour.
Could: I can use the process to make dyes of a desired shade.

Introduction
Invite children to look at their own clothes and find out what materials they are made from e.g. cotton, polyester, nylon etc. Elicit where these materials are sourced and sort into sets: man-made and natural.

Draw their attention to the colour of a material e.g. a white cotton shirt and enquire whether cotton is always that colour.

Discuss and elicit that we dye materials to change their colour.

Main Teaching

Explain how for thousands of years, dyes were made using natural materials like leaves, flowers, roots and bark. While these dyes were often very beautiful it was difficult to colour match them or repeat because there were so many variables involved in the process e.g. raw materials, climate and soil quality. With improved techniques and advances in chemistry most fabrics today are dyed using synthetic dyes. These create reliable results and are easy to colour match. Compare similar items.

Focus on natural dyes and the history of dyeing during Anglo Saxon Britain. Common materials used for dying were madder and woad. Madder gave a rich red pigment. Woad was the Anglo-Saxon source of indigo blue (see Facts for Teacher).

Consider the science behind it. Natural dyes will only dye natural materials. Natural materials can be categorised into groups: vegetable materials (e.g. cotton, flax, hemp, jute and linen) and protein materials (e.g. wool, mohair, cashmere and silk). Explain how natural dyes bond better with protein materials, which is why yarn dyeing is such a successful and ancient practice. Traditionally yarn was woven into skeins of yarn to make it more workable (see Facts for Teacher). Display some dyestuff and ask the children what colours of dye they think they will make.

Choose turmeric or tea/coffee and model the task:
How to extract a dye (Use an Instruction Card)
1. Sprinkle enough turmeric into a saucepan of water to cover the base.
2. Bring the water to the boil and then allow it to simmer.
3. Add 2 tsp. of the mordant.
4. Stir until the turmeric and the mordant are almost dissolved.
5. Leave it to cool and settle for a while.
6. Then strain or filter the solution. Explain how the mordant helps fix the dye to the yarn or fabric.

Model the second task: Dyeing the yarn
1. Immerse the skein of wool in the dye bath.
2. Return to the heat for 30 minutes.
3. Leave to cool.
4. Remove the skein of wool and hang to dry.

Explain how there needs to be an increase in temperature in order for the dye and the yarn to bond.

Elicit how the strength or shade of the colour might be enhanced e.g. amount of dye used or length of time in dyebath.

Teacher Led and Independent Group Tasks

Remind the children about how to be safe in the kitchen when working with sharp tools, hot plates and hot water. Have five dyeing stations previously set up with instruction cards and all the necessary produce for the task. Organise the children to work in mixed ability groups, each at a dyeing station, with an adult. Draw attention to the choice of other essentials placed centrally e.g. strainer, colander, filter paper, skeins of yarn etc.
Set the tasks: Task 1. Make a dye bath. Task 2. Dye the yarn.

Extension

With three skeins of yarn per group, using one at a time, can you intensify the colour between the skeins?

Plenary (AfL Focus)

Share the learning experience: Encourage the groups to talk through their experience of making dyes. Consider the colours they have created. Were there any surprises? Are the skeins likely to change colour while drying? Enquire how they experimented to vary the colours e.g. vary the amount of dye or water, the amount of time in the dyebath or the temperature of dye. Discuss. Revisit the learning objective and self assess their learning using Steps to Success.

Next Steps/Home Learning

Art & Design: Use the newly dyed yarn to yarn wrap landscapes or seascapes. Weave a class wall hanging showing gradation of colours.

Home Learning: Consider the clothes you wear and whether natural produce might have been used to dye them.

Resources/Facts for the Teacher

Suitable dyestuff (beetroot, red cabbage, onion skins, berries (blueberries, blackberries, raspberries), spinach, coffee, tea, turmeric, alum powder, stainless steel or enamel pots, strainers, colanders, filter papers, cutting utensils and chopping boards, utensils to stir, tongs, aprons, rubber gloves, Dyebath Instruction Cards, 100g skeins of white/ natural wool yarn, weighing scales and measuring jugs.

Exemplar Instruction Cards:
How to make a dye bath from red cabbage:
Chop a whole red cabbage, Place it in a saucepan of water (approx. 1l) on a hot plate. Bring it to the boil and simmer for approx. 20 minutes. Stir occasionally. Allow it to cool. Mash it with a potato masher to extract more colour. Sieve to separate and create the dyebath.

How to dye a skein of yarn:
Return the dyebath to the heat. Add the mordant (a small sachet of alum powder/2 teaspoons). Stir. Immerse the wool skein in the dyebath for 30 minutes or longer. Allow to cool. Remove and hang to dry. Extension: Using another skein of yarn, can you intensify the colour?

Proposed amounts if using these dye stuff as above.
Beetroot: 500g peeled and chopped, as above.
Spinach: 500g chopped, as above
Onion skins: use the peeled skins from some 6/8 onions.

How to make a dye bath from berries:
Use berries (blueberries, blackberries, raspberries, blackcurrants). Put the berries in a saucepan of water (approx. 1l) over heat. Bring to the boil and simmer for 30 minutes. Stir and crush occasionally with the back of a spoon. Allow to cool. Mash to extract more colour. Sieve to separate and create the dyebath. Return the dyebath to the heat. Add the mordant (a small sachet of alum powder/2 tsp.). Stir. Immerse the wool skein in the dyebath for 30 minutes or longer. Allow to cool. Remove and hang to dry.

A dye is a pigment, natural or synthetic, used to change the colour of something. Natural dyes come from plant sources. Synthetic dyes are man-made dyes.

Research into what Anglo-Saxons wore suggests that dyes were only used during the later Anglo-Saxon era. Shades of yellow, blue and brown were more common when dyeing garments while reds and purples were reserved for the rich and noble and if used by common folk were only used for accessories like head dresses, bags and embroidery threads. Madder is one of the most ancient dyes. The roots of the plant are a rich red pigment. Madder was popular during Roman Britain and during the later Anglo-Saxon era. Woad is a flowering plant (it belongs to the broccoli and cauliflower family) and it gives its name to the blue dye made from the leaves of the plant. A mordant permanently bonds dye pigments to fabrics. It causes a chemical reaction, which creates a new colour. Table salt can be used as a mordant. Alum powder, as a mordent, is the easiest and safest mordant to use. Yarn is a continuous strand of twisted threads used for knitting or weaving e.g. wool and nylon. Skein of yarn is a loosely wrapped coil of yarn, which can be made using an extra pair of hands.

Maths
English
MFL: Mandarin
D&T

Year 6 Lesson Overview

Subject	Learning Objectives	Curriculum Links	Cross Curricular Links	Page Numbers
Maths Gingerbread Pyramids	To measure angles.	**Ma6/3.2 Properties of Shape** Ma6/3.2c compare and classify geometric shapes based on their properties and sizes and find unknown angles in any triangles, quadrilaterals, and regular polygons	History English D&T: Cooking & Nutrition	114, 115, 116
English Egyptian Retelling	To write a recount.	**En3/3.3 Composition** En3/3.3a Plan their writing by: -discussing writing similar to that which they are planning to write in order to understand and learn from its structure, vocabulary and grammar -discussing and recording ideas En3/3.3b Draft and write in non-narrative material, using simple organisational devices En3/3.3c Evaluate and edit by: assessing the effectiveness of their own and others' writing and suggesting improvements	History D&T: Cooking and Nutrition	117, 118, 119
MFL: Mandarin Chinese Food	To describe food from another culture.	**Key stage 2: Foreign language** Pupils should be taught to: — Engage in conversations; ask and answer questions; express opinions and respond to those of others; seek clarification and help. — Speak in sentences, using familiar vocabulary, phrases and basic language structures. — Describe people, places, things and actions orally and in writing.	English	120, 121, 122

Subject	Learning Objectives	Curriculum Links	Cross Curricular Links	Page Numbers
D&T Chicken Coup	To design and make a prototype for a chicken coup.	**DT2/1.1 Design** DT2/1.1a use research and develop design criteria to inform the design of innovative, functional, appealing products that are fit for purpose, aimed at particular individuals or groups. DT2/1.1b generate, develop, model and communicate their ideas through discussion, annotated sketches, cross-sectional and exploded diagrams, prototypes, pattern pieces and computer-aided design. **DT2/1.2 Make** DT2/1.2a select from and use a wider range of tools and equipment to perform practical tasks accurately. **DT2/1.3 Evaluate** DT2/1.3a investigate and analyse a range of existing products DT2/1.3b evaluate their ideas and products against their own design criteria and consider the views of others to improve their work **DT2/1.4 Technological Knowledge** DT2/1.4a apply their understanding of how to strengthen, stiffen and reinforce more complex structures	Information Communication Technology, Science, D&T: Cooking & Nutrition	123, 124, 125

Year 6 Maths Lesson
Gingerbread Pyramids

Theme/Unit
Ancient Egypt

Lesson Overview
Children to apply their understanding of angles and skills in measuring angles, to create triangular based pyramids.

Previous Learning
Maths: Triangles and their properties.
D&T: Cooking & Nutrition: Make gingerbread and keep refrigerated.

Learning Objective
To measure angles accurately.

Success Criteria
Must: I can measure angles accurately.
Should: I know that the three angles inside a triangle always add up to 180°.
Could: I can draw and make congruent triangles.

Introduction
Begin asking the children: What are angles? How are they measured? What is the symbol for degrees? Using their WBs can they draw an angle? Can they name it?

Display examples and through questioning revisit the characteristics of each angle i.e. acute, obtuse and reflex and ensure the children are confident naming them (see web links).

Show an equilateral triangle on the IWB. Ask: What type of triangle is it? Elicit its properties. What would each angle measure? Can you explain how you know? Similarly show an isosceles triangle with one angle measurement included at the base. Can they name the triangle and work out the measurements for the other two angles? Continue, showing a scalene triangle, giving two angle measurements.

Establish that the three angles inside a triangle always add up to 180°.

Main Teaching

Ask how we would measure the angles accurately if we didn't have any measurements to work from. Elicit using a protractor and explain how we can see whether it is an acute or obtuse angle but we need a protractor to measure accurately. Distribute some protractors and elicit children's previous experience of using them. Demonstrate how to measure angles using an interactive protractor on the IWB (see web links).

Line up the protractor so the 'cross hair' is exactly on the vertex of the angle. Explain that the vertex is the point where the two rays of the angle meet. Rotate the protractor so the horizontal black line with the 0 is directly on top of one of the rays. Read the scale along which the other ray runs to measure the angle. If it is between 50 and 60, the angle must be fifty something degrees. Count the small degrees up from 50 to measure the angle accurately.

Top Tip: Whether you read the top scale or the bottom scale depends on the orientation of the protractor so always check if it is an acute (less than 90 °) or obtuse (greater than 90 °) angle before beginning.

Mini Activity: Distribute activity sheets with angles to measure. Encourage children to practise measuring angles using protractors. Compare results and strategies.

Teacher Led and Independent Group Tasks

Show a picture of the Pyramids at Giza and ask how the Ancients Egyptians built them so accurately. How did they measure the angles? Show a picture of an Egyptian level-square, used to measure angles. Explain simply how it was used (see web links).

Explain the task: To make a triangular based pyramid from gingerbread. Begin by looking at and handling 3D triangular pyramids. Elicit properties: 4 faces, all triangles, 4 vertices, 6 edges. Establish all the triangles are the same and are equilateral. Question what they know about equilateral triangles, refer to earlier display model. Give each child a triangular prism net to cut out and fold to assemble. Explain that this will be their template for making their gingerbread pyramid. Ask what measurements they need from the template e.g. length of sides, angle measurements.

Record and discuss the next steps on the whiteboard:
— Take measurements from the template and record.
— Roll out the ginger bread on a floured surface.
— Use a ruler and protractor to make 4 equilateral triangles (to match measurements).
— Self-check gingerbread triangles with the template.
— Bake gingerbread triangles and leave to cool (approximately 30 minutes).

(BA) TA to work with this group. Reiterate the learning i.e. handle the pyramids, elicit the properties, look at the nets etc. Children to measure and record their measurements on their templates and follow the steps to making 4 equilateral triangles. TA to assist where necessary.

(A) These groups to work independently following the steps, to create their own equilateral triangles.

(HA)This group to work in pairs to create triangular pyramids double the size of the template. Teacher to work with this group. Look again at the triangular pyramids. Elicit the properties. Explain the term congruent (see Facts for Teacher).

Consider how to double the size of the template. Decide on the measurements. Create a template. Follow the steps to create 4 large equilateral triangles.

Plenary (AfL Focus)
Share the learning: Look at the templates and compare the sizes.
Ask:
Are all the triangles congruent?
What measuring skills did they use?
What did they find tricky?
What did they learn?

Revisit the learning objective and self assess their learning using Steps to Success.

Finally, consider the triangular pyramid— as a tetrahedron and a platonic solid (see web links).

Next Steps/Home Learning
Maths: Using the cooled gingerbread triangles, assemble a pyramid on a paper plate with icing and compare with original templates.
Find the surface area and/or volume of the finished pyramids.
Home Learning: Consider angles when cutting pizza/ cake for the family.

Resources/Facts for the Teacher
WBs and pens, IWB, pictures of the various triangles and angles to display, rulers, protractors, teaching protractor, mini activity measuring angle sheets, 3D triangular pyramids, 3D triangular pyramid nets, ginger bread, rolling pins, flour, icing, chopping boards, cutting tools, paper plates, oven.

Equilateral triangle has 3 equal sides and 3 equal angles (each 60°). Isosceles triangle has 2 equal sides, 2 equal angles (base angles). Scalene triangle has all different sides and all different angles.

Right Angle triangle has one 90° angle and the two other angles add up to 90°. The longest side is the hypotenuse.

In any triangle the sum of the angles is 180°.
Angles are a measure of turn.
They are measured in degrees.
The symbol for degrees is °.
A whole turn measures 360°.
   A half turn measures 180° and is a straight line.
A quarter turn is 90°or a right angle.
An angle measuring less than 90° is an acute angle.
An angle measuring between 90° and 180° is obtuse.
An angle measuring greater than 180° is a reflex angle.
Congruent: In geometry when two or more triangles are congruent they have exactly the same three sides and exactly the same threes angles.
Tetrahedron is another name for a triangular pyramid. They both have the same properties.

A Platonic Solid is a 3D shape where all the faces are the same regular polygon and there are the same numbers of polygons meeting at each vertex.

Year 6 English Lesson
Egyptian Retelling

Theme/Unit
Ancient Egypt

Lesson Overview
Imagine you witnessed a 'Weighing of the Heart Ceremony' write a recount of the event.

Previous Learning
English: Know features of a recount.
History: Learn about mummification.

Learning Objective
To write a recount.

Success Criteria
Must: I can retell an event in chronological order.
Should: I can make it lively and interesting.
Could: I can add some reflection.

Introduction
Revisit the children's understanding of mummification through questioning. Elicit how the heart is not removed from the body (see Facts for Teacher).

Explain how the ancient Egyptians believed in a ritual called the 'Weighing of the Heart Ceremony'. Show an ox heart and some scales. Estimate the weight. Have some children weigh the heart. Discuss.

Show a feather, estimate the weight and have some children weigh it. Compare the weights.

Main Teaching

Show a picture of the 'Weighing of the Heart Ceremony' on the IWB to show the presence of the heart and the feather. Explain the significance of the ritual as the soul's journey to the afterlife (see web links). Introduce the place, the characters and their roles.

Create a tableau, inviting children to assume the various roles, as depicted in the picture. Call this group A. Label accordingly: The deceased, Anubis, Thoth, Horus, Osiris, Ammit, fellow men x 9. Explain the ceremony chronologically (see Facts for Teacher). Invite questions. Next encourage group A to re-enact the 'Weighing of the Heart Ceremony' of the Pharaoh while group B (the other half of the class) take turns to narrate what is happening. Together evaluate the narration on the IWB. Elicit improvements e.g. action verb - Ammit is drooling in anticipation.

Structure	Language
Introduction (What and why)	correct tense
involve everyone	action verbs
chronological order	third person (impersonal)
other details	connectives
closing statment	names of people and places

Swap roles: group B to re-enact the ceremony while group A narrate what is happening. Encourage the children to extend their learning: Can they use more interesting verbs? Can they add a closing statement to sum up the main points?

Evaluate group B's narration using all the criteria. Through questioning ensure the children clearly understand the 'Weighing of the Heart Ceremony'.

Teacher Led and Independent Group Tasks

Imagine you were an observer at the 'Weighing of the Heart Ceremony' of the Pharaoh. Retell what happened. You can decide how the ceremony ends. Remember you were there as an observer so should be detached.

(BA) TA to work with this group to encourage them to recount what happened at the 'Weighing of the Heart Ceremony' of the Pharaoh. Use questions and picture clues to stimulate their retelling. Elicit the tense they should use. Build up a word bank of names of people and places, action verbs and connectives before they begin their retelling. Assist where necessary.

(A) These groups can work independently to retell, in a lively and interesting way, what happened at the 'Weighing of the Heart Ceremony' from the point of view of an observer who was there e.g. The Pharaoh strode regally... The scales teetered ominously ... Encourage the children to begin with an introduction explaining what is happening and why, to refer to the pictures of the ceremony, to consider the tense before beginning, to use the names of places and people on display and to include connectives and action verbs.

(HA) Teacher to work with this group, as above, but to further extend their learning by encouraging them to add some personal reflection on what they witnessed e.g. I thought ... and a closing statement to sum up the recount.

Plenary (AfL Focus)

Encourage children to share their recounts. Revisit the learning objective and self assess their learning using Steps to Success. Watch film on the Weighing of the Heart Ceremony (see web links).

Next Steps/Home Learning

D&T: Cooking & Nutrition: Re-weigh the heart. Demonstrate how to cut it. Children to grill it while other groups prepare salad and flatbreads to accompany it.
Home Learning: Retell what happened at the Weighing of the Heart Ceremony in Ancient Egypt.

Resources/Facts for the Teacher

Images of the Weighing of the Heart Ceremony, IWB, ox heart, feather, weighing scales, character and place name cards.

A tableau: a group of motionless figures representing a scene from a story or from history.

The ancient Egyptians believed that after death they would have a new kind of life called the afterlife. As well as needing all their everyday possessions for the next life, they also needed their bodies and so they were mummified after they died. They believed the heart was the place where a person's emotions, intellect, will and morality lived. One could not have an afterlife without it so during mummification the heart was left in the body. To enter the afterlife, they believed you had to have a light heart.

You gained a light heart by doing many good deeds during your lifetime. They believed that after you died, on your way to your afterlife, your heart had to be weighed against the 'Feather of Truth and Justice'. First the deceased had to plead their innocence to the Gods and fellow men. Then the god Anubis would lead them through the Hall of Maat where Osiris presided over the ceremony.

The god Anubis would weigh the deceased's heart. The god Thoth would record the findings. Ammit, the demon with the crocodile head and lion and hippo shaped body, would wait nearby. If the heart was as a light as a feather, the deceased passed Maat's test, and was led by Horus to Osiris, who was seated nearby on the Throne of Maat. Horus would tell Osiris that the deceased had passed the weighing of the heart.
The god Osiris would open the door to the afterlife for the deceased.

The ancient Egyptians believed if the heart was heavy, it was because the deceased did something really bad during their lifetime and so the demon Ammit would magically appear and devour them. The deceased would then die a second time and not gain eternity in the afterlife.

Year 6 MFL: Mandarin Lesson
Chinese Food

Theme/Unit
Made in China

Lesson Overview
To learn to express opinions in Mandarin while preparing and reviewing Chinese food.

Previous Learning
English: Visit a Chinese restaurant and write a restaurant review.
D&T: Cooking and Nutrition: Research a dish to prepare and cook. Plan a shopping list.
MFL: Mandarin: Learn vocabulary for healthy foods. Sentences: What do you like to eat? I like...

Learning Objective
To describe food from another culture.

Success Criteria
Must: I know some Chinese foods.
Should: I can express simple opinions about them.
Could: I can use sentences to describe how they look and taste.

Introduction
Play quick recall while displaying some mandarin flash cards (images and words) of healthy food e.g. fruit and vegetables.

Revisit the sentences: Nǐ xǐhuān chī shénme? 你想吃什么？(What do you like to eat?) , Wǒ xǐhuān... 我喜欢 (I like...) Record on sentence strips. Children to repeat the phrases and add their food preferences. Display.

Play a circular table game: Teacher says Wǒ xǐhuān...我喜欢 (I like...) choosing a food and then turns to the next person saying Nǐ xǐhuān chī shénme? 你想吃什么？(What do you like to eat?) and so on around the table.

Main Teaching

In the kitchen consider the dishes the groups have chosen to prepare and the ingredients they have gathered for each dish. Can the children name the dishes? Show cards with the images. Show flash cards with the corresponding words. Model saying the words. Can the children match the words to the images saying the words?

Can the children name the ingredients? Can they describe them? (colour, number) Refer to a Mandarin colour and number chart on display. Introduce and display sentence strips saying 'Wǒ xǐhuān... 我喜欢 (I like...)' and 'Wǒ bù xǐhuān... 我不喜欢 (I don't like...)'. Model saying the phrases and encourage the children to repeat them. Can they sort some of the ingredients into 'like' and 'don't like' sets while saying the appropriate sentence?

Introduce some 'taste' phrases (on sentence strips) e.g.
Tā wèidào tián 它味道甜 (It tastes sweet)
Tā wèidào suān 它味道酸 (It tastes sour)
Tā wèidào xián wèi 它味道咸 (It tastes salty)
Tā wèidào là 它味道辛辣 (It tastes spicy)

Model speaking each of the phrases. Look for common words. Identify the different taste words. Encourage the children to practise saying them to each other.

Present a selection of chopped ingredients e.g. apple, red onion, carrot, red pepper and green pepper. Ask some children to taste and sort the ingredients into the above categories saying the appropriate sentence. Display.

Children to prepare their chosen dishes in groups e.g. chūn juǎn 春卷 (spring rolls), chǎo miàn 炒面(chow mein), gǔ lǎo ròu 古老肉 (sweet and sour pork), dàn chǎo fàn 蛋炒饭 (egg fried rice), gōngbǎo jīdīng 宫保鸡丁 (kung pao chicken).

Remind them about safety and hygiene when preparing food. Encourage them to name the ingredients as they cut, chop, snip and cook. TA to supervise the hot plate cooking. Teacher to move between the groups, helping where necessary and taking photographs of the finished dishes.

Teacher Led and Independent Group Tasks

Introduce the proposed activity as planning a food review of their Chinese dish.

Can the children name their Chinese food and its ingredients? Show the flashcards with the images again and those with the corresponding words. Can the children match the words to the images?

Encourage them to taste their dish. What does it taste like? Refer to the earlier display of flash cards and phrases, e.g.
Wǒ xǐhuān gǔ lǎo ròu 我喜欢古老肉 (I like sweet and sour pork)
Tā wèidào tián 它味道甜 (It tastes sweet)
Tā wèidào suān 它味道酸 (It tastes sour)

Begin to build a word bank on the WB of other words and phrases the children use.

Task: Children to work in talking pairs to practise speaking their reviews. Encourage them to use the resources on display and to speak in sentences. Teacher and TA can offer help when needed.

Plenary (AfL Focus)
Listen to each other's spoken reviews. Consider the children's likes and dislikes and which dishes tasted sweet, sour, savoury and spicy. Revisit the learning objective and self assess their learning using Steps to Success. Play Matching Pairs Food Game with the new vocabulary (names of Chinese dishes) and the corresponding images.

Extension
Consider playing a game, matching foods with corresponding tastes.

Next Steps/Home Learning
MFL: Mandarin: Use the class word bank and new phrases to recall and then write a review of your Chinese dish.
Home Learning: Plan and help prepare a Chinese meal for the family. Play the food and drink game (see web links).

Resources/Facts for the Teacher
Picture Flash Cards (images of fruit, vegetables, Chinese dishes and ingredients), Word flash Cards (with the corresponding words), sentences strips, Mandarin Number Chart, Mandarin Colour Chart, selection of foods to taste, ingredients, recipes, kitchen equipment and appliances.

Online references see web links.

Health benefits of Chinese Food
Chinese philosophers, Confucius and Taoism, not only contributed to philosophy but also to the way the Chinese food is prepared and served. Chinese food is about small bite size pieces and a combination of herbs, condiments, colour and texture. Chinese food is prepared and cooked with the intention of promoting longevity and healing power, so food is thought of as medicine. Emphasis in meals is on the rice, noodles and vegetables. Eating meals rich in vegetables provides a range of plant chemicals (phytonutrients), which offer an array of protective health benefits to the body. Dishes tend to be steamed or stir-fried.

This lesson could be adapted for another language.

Year 6 D&T Lesson
Chicken Coup

Theme/Unit
Living Things and their Habitats

Lesson Overview
To consider the welfare of chickens by designing a newly improved chicken coup

Previous Learning
Science: Living Things and their Habitats: classifying species according to their characteristics.
D&T: Focused Practical Tasks: experiment and learn a variety of ways to strengthen and join materials.

Learning Objective
To design and make a prototype for a chicken coup.

Success Criteria
Must: I can talk about aspects of my design and plan a course of action to model it.
Should: I can carefully apply my practical skills when modelling.
Could: I can evaluate my design for strengths and areas of improvement.

Introduction
If you have chickens at your school take a walk outside to the garden to look more closely at the chickens in their chicken coup. If not watch a film of chickens on the IWB. Consider how content they are.

Elicit what the children already know about chickens e.g. they belong to the bird family (see Facts for Teacher).

Look for freshly laid eggs and collect. Discuss various aspects of their man-made habitat: What materials are used to build a coup? How is it made? Why has it been made this way? What are the different parts called? What is each section for? Could the habitat be improved?

Main Teaching

Introduce the children to the challenge: How can we design a better habitat for chickens?

Listen to children's initial ideas before introducing the research project. Suggest children work in small groups (mixed ability) to investigate the range of coups available to buy. Before beginning, elicit what attributes they think would make a good chicken coup e.g. Does it have a shelter? It is warm and dry? Is there easy access for chickens and baby chicks? What materials are used? Is there space for a run? Is it secure? Provide a range of sources of information: books, magazines, catalogues, diagrams and the Internet. Groups to record their attributes in a labelled diagram, information table or other format.

Reconvene and consider their findings e.g. waterproofed roof, ventilation holes, nesting box, cleaning tray etc. Having considered the various models and their attributes elicit the children's own initial ideas on designing a shelter for chickens. Ask: What features must it have? What else could it have? What shape would it be? What materials could be used?

Encourage groups to work as teams (discuss ideas, agree on a plan, allocate tasks etc.) and draw annotated sketches and/or labelled diagrams of their ideas.
Points to consider as they create their design:
— What resources are available
— The sequence of construction
— Techniques they may need to use when making their design.

Teacher and Teaching Assistant to move between the groups, asking questions and assisting where necessary.

Once complete share the designs. Encourage the groups to talk through their designs, the materials they will use, where they will begin and some of the practical techniques they will need to employ. Introduce some practical skills tasks and ask children to demonstrate their practical skills e.g. using a glue gun safely, strengthening a corner using triangles (see Facts for Teacher).

Teacher Led and Independent Group Tasks

Make a model of your ideal chicken coup. Each group to make a model of their coup design using the materials available: card, paper straws, plastic containers, netting etc. and their practical skills. Remind the groups to allocate tasks before beginning.

> Points to consider as a group
> How can we best join materials?
> How can we make the structure stand up?
> How can we make it more stable?
> How can we reinforce weaker points?
> If a first attempt fails we try an alternative way.

↓   ↓   ↓

> Points to evaluate as the group progresses
> Will it make a good chicken coup?
> Is it spacious?
> Is it cosy?
> Is it accessible?
> It is secure?

Teacher to supervise the use of the glue gun and Teaching Assistant to supervise the cutting area.

Plenary (AfL Focus)

Share the learning: Each group to present their design and communicate its attributes. Take photographs. Encourage the children to evaluate each other's designs. Revisit the learning objective and self assess their learning using Steps to Success.

Discuss with the children what they have learnt and elicit some targets for making a more robust model. Show some eggs collected from the chicken coup. Ask the children what their favourite egg dishes to prepare and eat are.

Next Steps/Home Learning

D&T: Cooking and Nutrition: Use eggs to prepare some healthy egg dishes e.g. boil, scramble, fry or poach the eggs.
English: Design a bill board advertisement/radio advertisement to market your chicken coup design.
Home Learning: Consider other habitats in your neighbourhood e.g. a woodland or a pond. What is their purpose? Do they do what they are intended to do? Could they be improved?

Resources/Facts for the Teacher

Sources of information (catalogues, magazines, leaflets, books, Internet), A3 paper for annotated designs, modelling materials (glue, glue gun, split pins, treasury tags, sticky tape, paper, paper straws, card, corrugated card, triangular corners, plastic trays and containers, clear plastic sheets, netting, pulley mechanisms, doweling, pieces of wood, lollipop sticks, waterproof fabrics, string) cutting tools and cutting boards.

Chickens belong to the bird family. Like all birds they have feathers, wings and two legs. They have ear holes instead of ears. They are warm blooded so they can keep themselves warm. They lay eggs. Some scientists believe they may have descended from dinosaurs.

A habitat is a place where plants and animals live and it provides them with food and shelter.

Some features of a chicken coup: waterproof roof, secure door, nesting box, windows for ventilation and natural light, ventilation grills, ramp with gripping material, slide out cleaning tray.

Practical skills

— Techniques for reinforcing and strengthening structures e.g. adding diagonals or triangles.

— Test how the use of a textiles cover can strengthen a structure.

— Provide a range of fixatives and experiment with different methods of joining materials e.g. plastic and paper, square and rectangular sections of wood, fabric and wood, doweling etc.

Beyond the classroom

— After school clubs. Charlton Manor provides several after school clubs including parents/carers and children cooking together, studying different countries and cultures through food, supporting fussy eaters, nutrition advice and teaching cooking skills. There is also gardening and bee keeping club as well as recycling or up cycling club and craft club.

— Community Garden. Having a community garden provides a wonderful resource to take food growing to a new dimension. It allows growing of produce on a scale that can be sold at a school shop, used in school lunches and can support a school teaching kitchen. It can also provide produce for local restaurants. Parents like to volunteer to help in these areas and this can be of benefit through the holidays including during holiday hunger programmes.

— School Shop. This provides a great resource for pupils to embed Maths and English as well as provide a wonderful community hub. Children work on developing products that sell well and are healthy. Products such as reduced sugar beetroot cake, fruit and vegetables, honey, eggs to such things as recycled pallets built into plant boxes, bird boxes or bug hotels.

— Cookery and Bread making classes. Classes can be run at weekends so that anyone can access them. Outside providers can deliver these sessions, which can further support school food culture.

Connections

— Local Housing Association. A great way to provide more learning opportunities for the children is to connect with others in the community.

— Local Football Club. Space at local Football grounds can provide an area for growing food and cookery/nutrition sessions can be delivered at local clubs. This also supports the importance placed on the food agenda by the school and supports the community making a link between exercise and nutrition.

— Local Restaurants. These links can support understanding foods from around the World and the related customs and traditions as well as a link to RE. Children can also learn about waiting on tables, cooking, taking orders, advertising and pricing as well as sourcing produce.

— Local Supermarkets. Supermarkets provide several opportunities for food education from tours of the store to identify different fruits and vegetables, looking at labelling to links with farms supplying the produce. They can also support the school through donations for things like breakfast club or after school clubs as well as providing money for specific projects.

— Links abroad. Activities abroad can provide the children with incredible learning opportunities. At Charlton Manor we have links with schools, farms and organisations in Germany, France, China, Nepal and Dubai. These links also include visits for staff and pupils. Our work with Dubai has helped the children at Charlton Manor understand the complexity of food and the importance of eating healthily. They have a whole community approach to tackling obesity from schools and hospitals to provision in restaurants and fast food outlets.

Working with parents

The activities already described involve the parents but some particular ones follow.

Homework

Many of the lessons have a suggested home learning activity or task around food to complete. This could be a recipe to follow or things to look out for when food shopping such as labels, sugar content, salt content etc. Encouraging communication around food at home not only creates an interest in what they eat but can also promote and enhance positive relationships with parents or carers.

Added to this parents or carers that may struggle with traditional school work can complete homework when its centered around food or cooking, or are more comfortable asking at school for support, whether following instructions, weighing and measuring, fractions, ratio and proportions, following clues or a news story about food provenance. Food provides the perfect vehicle to drive homework bringing all the family into the food discussion.

Social Media

There is no doubt that social media is a great way to engage children. Charlton Manor has its own YouTube channel. On this the children broadcast cookery lessons. They plan, script and prepare for the program in which they demonstrate and describe the cooking of healthy meals. This not only supports their cooking skills, knowledge, confidence, script writing, descriptive language and Maths but also provides useful material on the channel that can be used at home to encourage healthy eating. The children frequently go home and get their families to cook the recipes by following it on their PCs.

Morning Circuits

Charlton Manor run a daily morning circuit session for the pupils and parents. It runs for 30mins from 8.25am. Others from outside the school also attend.

How Charlton Manor can Support You
Charlton Manor has a staff team of experts that teach
through food on a daily basis. This support can be
accessed by other schools through training events
and an annual conference delivered at the school.

The Head Teacher is very proactive about sharing their
success and is available to speak at conferences, events
and to other schools.

Please contact the school directly to discuss your needs
further.

www.charltonmanorprimary.co.uk
Email: admin@charltonmanor.greenwich.sch.uk
Phone: 020 8856 6525

How The Food Teacher can Support You
As The Food Teacher, Katharine works with schools
in various ways depending on staff and pupil needs,
funding and priority.

Katharine has extensive experience working with schools
offering advisory support, reviewing school catering,
developing curriculum content, policy development,
talks/workshops for parents and staff, mentoring staff
and model and team teaching. Measuring the impact of
her support is an inclusive aspect of her work.

Katharine has also written the award-winning book **'No
Kitchen Cookery for Primary Schools'.** Available through
her website and Amazon.

Please contact The Food Teacher to discuss
your needs further.
www.thefoodteacher.co.uk
Email: info@thefoodteacher.co.uk

No Kitchen Cookery
For Primary Schools
Katharine Tate

Simple recipes for Key Stage 1 and 2 that deliver
the Cooking and Nutrition Curriculum (2014) within the classroom

'No Kitchen Cookery' has been designed for schools
with limited or no kitchen access to deliver as aspect of
the Cooking and Nutrition National Curriculum for Key
Stage 1 and 2 within classrooms. **'No Kitchen Cookery'**
aims to give teachers an outline for cookery lessons
with objectives, outcomes and assessment opportunites
clearly identified and provides easy to follow recipes.

DUMP THE JUNK — BE SUGAR SMART!

**SUGAR
SMART**

SMART KIDS ARE SUGAR SMART.

**SUGAR
SMART**

Lightning Source UK Ltd.
Milton Keynes UK
UKHW051303120919
349642UK00001B/3/P